Unshackled

Unleashing the Power Within to Overcome Self-Doubt

KP Akom

Copyright © 2023 by KP Akom

Contents

INTRODUCTION 1
A Journey of Transformation and Empowerment

PART I: THE STRUGGLE 4

CHAPTER 1 5
A New Beginning - Embracing the Unknown in a New World

CHAPTER 2 10
The Daily Grind - Finding Strength in the Face of Adversity

PART II: TURNING POINTS 16

CHAPTER 3 17
Acknowledging Her Feelings - Embracing the Reality of Self-Doubt

CHAPTER 4 23
Identifying the Source of Her Doubt - The Quest for Self-Understanding and Divine Guidance

CHAPTER 5 29
The Power of Self-Compassion - Cultivating Kindness Within

CHAPTER 6 38
The Power of Celebrating Successes - Recognizing Every Victory, Big or Small

CHAPTER 7 47
Unleashing Faith - Jennie-Lou's Journey to Conquer Self-Doubt

CHAPTER 8 53
Taking Action - Small Steps to Overcoming Self-Doubt and Achieving Greatness

CHAPTER 9 — 59
Embracing Accountability - The Power of Mentoring and Personal Growth

PART III: PURSUING HER DREAMS — 67

CHAPTER 10 — 68
A Bold Leap - The Emotional Rollercoaster of Jennie-Lou's First Attempt at Real Estate

CHAPTER 11 — 74
Resilience Awakened - Unveiling the Passion for Mid-Term Rentals on an Emotional Expedition

CHAPTER 12 — 84
Unleashing Possibilities: Rising Above Doubts and Discovering Financial Freedom Through Mid-Term Rentals

PART IV: EMPOWERING TRANSFORMATION — 96

CHAPTER 13 — 97
The Power of Perseverance - Learning from the Journey

CHAPTER 14 — 104
Embracing Failure - Turning Setbacks into Stepping Stones

CHAPTER 15 — 109
Sharing the Light - Inspiring and Empowering Others through Jennie-Lou's Journey

CHAPTER 16 — 113
Advice for Others - Keys to Overcoming Obstacles and Achieving Success

CONCLUSION — 118
Embracing Your Journey and Inspiring Others

INTRODUCTION

A Journey of Transformation and Empowerment

Welcome to a story of transformation, resilience, and the unwavering determination of the mind. In the following pages, you will embark on a powerful journey, witnessing the life of Jennie-Lou as she confronts her self-doubt and rises above her circumstances to achieve her dreams. Her story is a testament to the boundless potential that resides within each of us, waiting to be unleashed. This is a tale of struggle, perseverance, and triumph.

Our story begins when Jennie-Lou is in her late twenties, standing on the precipice of a life-altering decision. She leaves behind the familiar confines of her home country, setting sail towards the United States in a quest for new beginnings and fresh opportunities. With each step she takes into this foreign land, she steps further into the labyrinth of her inner fears and self-doubt.

However, Jennie-Lou is not one to be easily daunted. She refuses to be shackled by her circumstances or let her fears dictate her destiny. Instead, she embarks on a transformative journey towards self-discovery, wrestling with her inner fears and comes out on top. Her story is one of resilience, personal growth, and the amazing power of believing in oneself.

Along her journey, Jennie-Lou experiences the exhilarating highs of success and the crushing lows of failure. She savors moments of pure joy and endures periods of despair. Yet, through the turbulent seas of life, she remains undaunted. Her spirit, resilient. Her resolve, unshakeable. This relentless pursuit of her dreams eventually leads her to the doors of real estate, setting the stage for her ascent towards success and financial freedom.

In this book, we will accompany Jennie-Lou on her incredible journey, witnessing her metamorphosis from a woman trapped in the shadows of self-doubt to a confident, successful, and empowered beacon of inspiration. Together, we will uncover profound insights on overcoming adversities, embracing personal growth, and tapping into our inner strength to achieve our dreams.

As you immerse yourself in this narrative, be prepared to be inspired, challenged, and ultimately empowered. This is not just the story of Jennie-Lou's victory over self-doubt; it is a call to arms for each of us to face our fears, harness our inner strength, and sculpt the life we desire and deserve. So, let us embark on this journey together and unleash the boundless potential that lies within us.

To your unlimited potential,

KP Akom

Part I: The Struggle

Chapter 1

A New Beginning - Embracing the Unknown in a New World

The warm golden sun of Los Angeles bathed Jennie-Lou's skin as she stepped out of LAX airport, her eyes wide with a thrilling blend of excitement and apprehension. The air was filled with the tantalizing aroma of food trucks parked nearby, a smoky blend of grilled meats, onions, and peppers, which instantly triggered her stomach to growl. Lively sounds— from car horns to animated conversations and laughter— filled the air like a symphony, each note a testament to the vibrant energy of the city that would become her new home. Leaving the comfort and familiarity of her home country behind, Jennie-Lou clutched the small locket containing a picture of her family, a poignant reminder of the sacrifices she was making to pursue a brighter future.

Jennie-Lou grew up in a quaint little town in Southeast Asia, surrounded by a loving community and close family. She spent her days playing volleyball with her siblings, climbing trees, and helping her mother in the kitchen, secretly trying to master her mother's secret recipe for chicken adobo. Her parents had always told her that she was destined for more, and she had listened, her dreams of a better life fostering a relentless ambition that couldn't be satisfied by the confines of her small-town life. Though rich in love and support, her homeland grappled with economic hardships that manifested in scarce job prospects, a meager quality of life, and increased criminal activity. Despite the uncertainties and challenges ahead, this insatiable desire for a brighter future ultimately led her to relocate to the United States.

The moment Jennie-Lou arrived in America, she was overwhelmed by many new experiences. She found herself at a bustling diner on her first night, surrounded by a dizzying array of unfamiliar foods and flavors. She ordered a hamburger, and as she took her first bite, the explosion of flavors—savory beef, tangy pickle, and creamy cheese—was unlike anything she had tasted before. She fumbled with her fork, her attempts to replicate the eating habits of the patrons around her ending in a cascade of laughter from a nearby table. The city's busy streets and different smells and sounds excited and disoriented her as she tried to find her place in this new world. She encountered fresh adventures, challenges, and opportunities for growth and self-discovery with every turn.

In the weeks following Jennie-Lou's arrival, she wrestled with the inevitable hurdles that accompanied such a dramatic shift in her life. The language barrier posed a significant hurdle as she struggled to find her way around. She often found herself resorting to a combination of broken English and expressive gestures to communicate. The cultural differences were, at times, bewildering, leading to humorous misunderstandings and awkward moments. "Can you tell me where the nearest bus stop is?" she asked a passerby hesitantly, her question met with a furrowed brow and a shrug.

Adjusting to the fast-paced lifestyle and individualistic nature of the United States proved challenging for Jennie-Lou, who was more accustomed to the collectivist culture of her home country. One day, in an attempt to adapt to the local customs, she decided to attend a baseball game, a sport she knew nothing about. She sat among the cheering crowd, completely lost but amused by the excitement around her. As she endeavored to build a new social network and adapt to novel social norms, she grappled with feelings of isolation and a yearning for the familiarity and sense of belonging she had left behind.

One night, alone in a tiny apartment room she shared with three other strangers, she picked up her phone and scrolled through pictures of her family. As she looked at the picture of her mother's bright smile, she could almost smell the comforting aroma of her mother's chicken adobo, feel the warmth of the tropical sun on her skin, and hear the laughter of her siblings playing in the background. "I miss my family and friends," she confided to her journal, her heart laden with homesickness.

Despite the initial excitement of her new surroundings, Jennie-Lou soon found herself besieged by self-doubt and anxiety. Leaving behind a stable job and comfortable life in her home country, she had placed all her hopes and dreams in this new chapter of her life. As she confronted the realities of her situation, such as finding suitable employment and securing stable housing, the weight of her decision began to weigh heavily on her, casting a shadow over her once-bright future.

In her darkest moments, Jennie-Lou's faith remained her guiding light. She found a small local church where she attended services every Sunday, her faith providing her with the strength she needed to persevere through her struggles. Deep down, she knew this move was crucial in her journey towards self-discovery and personal growth. She recognized that the challenges she faced were an essential part of her transformation and that it was only by confronting her fears and doubts that she could truly break free of the limitations that had held her back for so long.

Over time, Jennie-Lou became more comfortable in her new surroundings. She found joy in simple things, like the smell of freshly baked bread from a bakery near her apartment or the melody of a street musician's guitar echoing through the streets. She constantly looked for opportunities to learn and grow, pushing herself to step outside her comfort zone and embrace the challenges ahead. She forged connections with people from various backgrounds and immersed herself in the diverse tapestry of cultures and traditions that make up the vibrant city of Los Angeles.

Join us as we explore Jennie-Lou's journey, looking at her hardships, triumphs, and the unique path that brought her from a place of self-doubt to achieving great success.

CHAPTER 2

The Daily Grind - Finding Strength in the Face of Adversity

Jennie-Lou, a motivated woman in her late twenties, was no stranger to adversity, as she had long been acquainted with life's challenges. Raised in a modest household in her home country, she had watched her parents work tirelessly to keep their family afloat. These early years shaped her resilience and taught her the value of hard work. Her dad, a hardworking farmer, and her mother, a caring schoolteacher, instilled in her the importance of humility, perseverance, and kindness at a very young age. Jennie-Lou's strong sense of responsibility and empathy could be traced back to her childhood, where she often cared for her siblings while her parents worked.

At first, navigating her way through the city was a challenge. The city was like an ever-changing maze, with each turn revealing a new scene. One day, she found herself lost in the labyrinth of LA's streets. Just when she was about to give up and hail a cab, she realized she had been circling around her destination. With a laugh, she told herself, 'Well, at least I'm getting better at reading street signs.'

Despite her immense challenges, Jennie-Lou refused to succumb to despair. As a tenacious and inventive individual, she understood that to survive and flourish in this foreign world, she needed to muster the fortitude to keep going. Each daybreak, she would recall her parents' sacrifices, and this memory would bolster her resolve. With the sun's golden rays illuminating the city, Jennie-Lou arose with a rejuvenated sense of purpose, ready to face the day's challenges.

Jennie-Lou's savings steadily diminished as the days passed, and her financial burden grew heavier. Success remained elusive, despite her numerous job applications. The specter of homelessness and the anxiety of venturing into the unknown caused her to question the wisdom of leaving her homeland for uncharted territory. She grappled with feelings of self-doubt and fear, but she also knew that growth comes from discomfort.

"This is so much harder than I imagined," she sighed, wishing she had been better equipped to face the hurdles ahead.

On a cloudy afternoon, having submitted several job applications, Jennie-Lou set out for a long, contemplative walk. During her stroll, she received a call from a prospective employer she had interviewed with—the one opportunity she thought could transform her fortunes. Her heart sank as they informed her they had selected another candidate, wishing her luck in her job search. Tears flowed freely down her cheeks as she buckled under the weight of disappointment and frustration. Overcome with emotion, she dropped to her knees and cried out, "God, why am I going through this? I trust you too much to fail." She whispered a prayer and dried her tears.

At that moment, she made a conscious choice. She chose to see this not as a rejection of her worth, but as a redirection towards a better opportunity. This was not failure; it was a moment of growth. Gradually, she grew attuned to the city's heartbeat, her days awash with the clamor of traffic, the murmur of conversation, and the labyrinthine network of streets and alleys crisscrossing Los Angeles. She persisted in applying for jobs and eventually secured a position as a grocery delivery driver. The work was demanding and the hours long, but it afforded her a steady income and a semblance of stability amidst the turmoil.

As Jennie-Lou navigated the intricacies of her new job and personal life, each day ushered in fresh challenges and vexations. The relentless hours and mounting stress left her physically and emotionally depleted, and the burden of her responsibilities seemed insurmountable. However, amidst these hardships, she discovered a wellspring of inner fortitude and resilience she never knew she had. Jennie-Lou's warm-hearted nature and genuine interest in the lives of others endeared her to her customers, who frequently expressed their gratitude for her indefatigable efforts.

Delivering groceries became more than a means of survival; it also gave Jennie-Lou invaluable life lessons. As she journeyed through the city streets, she learned the significance of patience and perseverance when facing adversity. Additionally, her countless interactions with customers provided insights into the lives and struggles of others, reminding her that she wasn't alone in her journey.

One day, she met an older woman whose warm smile and gentle demeanor left a lasting impression on Jennie-Lou. As Jennie-Lou handed over the groceries, the woman said, "Thank you, dear. Life can be hard, but people like you make it easier." This encounter served as a potent reminder that even small acts of kindness could profoundly impact others. The woman's words resonated with Jennie-Lou, lifting her spirits and reigniting her determination to overcome her struggles.

During her time as a grocery delivery worker, Jennie-Lou's self-doubt and anxiety continued to plague her. The ever-present cloud of uncertainty that hung over her future often left her feeling overwhelmed and hopeless. However, she refused to allow these feelings to consume her. Instead, she recognized the need to confront her fears and doubts head-on and began to search for ways to overcome them.

Jennie-Lou's pursuit of self-improvement led her to immerse herself in the world of personal development, devouring books and attending workshops that provided her with the tools and strategies she needed to reshape her mindset and conquer her self-doubt. As she continued this journey of self-discovery, she noticed a shift in her perspective as the debilitating effects of her anxiety and depression slowly gave way to a newfound sense of hope and self-belief.

With each passing day, Jennie-Lou grew more resilient and resourceful, drawing on her inner strength and the wisdom she had acquired from her experiences. Her strong work ethic, unwavering determination, and ability to connect with others on a deeply personal level made her a force to be reckoned with, and she began to see the possibilities for her future expand.

Chapter 2 of Jennie-Lou's story is a testament to the power of persistence and the indomitable strength of the human spirit. In the face of seemingly insurmountable obstacles, she found the courage to keep moving forward, fueled by her unwavering faith and determination to create a better life for herself. Her experiences during this period laid the groundwork for the incredible transformation yet to come as she embarked on her path toward self-actualization and realizing her dreams.

Part II: Turning Points

CHAPTER 3

Acknowledging Her Feelings - Embracing the Reality of Self-Doubt

Growing up in a small town, Jennie-Lou was raised by her loving but overprotective parents. They instilled in her the importance of hard work, humility, and respecting authority. However, their cautious approach to life and fear of failure led Jennie-Lou to internalize the belief that she was never quite good enough. This manifested as self-doubt that followed her into adulthood.

Upon arriving in the United States, Jennie-Lou faced many new challenges, from cultural differences to language barriers. These issues made her feelings of not being good enough even stronger, making her question herself and her worth. But Jennie-Lou's strong will and determination kept her moving forward despite her internal struggles.

Jennie-Lou's personality was characterized by her compassionate heart, empathy for others, and unwavering sense of responsibility. Her self-doubt was partly fueled by her inability to acknowledge her needs and emotions. She was often the first to offer help or a listening ear but rarely allowed herself to be vulnerable and share her struggles.

As she began to take control of her life and work on her mindset, she realized that it was crucial to acknowledge her feelings and face her self-doubt head-on. Her desire for personal growth and a better life was a powerful motivator in confronting her fears.

Through journaling, Jennie-Lou explored her childhood experiences, societal pressures, and past failures that contributed to her self-doubt. She found solace in her faith, which not only provided her with spiritual strength but also helped her understand the value of embracing vulnerability and seeking support from others.

One evening, as Jennie-Lou was reading through her journal entries, she came across a verse from the Bible that struck a chord within her: "Be strong and courageous. Do not be afraid or terrified because of them, for the Lord your God goes with you; he will never leave you nor forsake you." (Deuteronomy 31:6). This verse reminded Jennie-Lou that she was never alone in her journey and that God was always by her side, guiding and providing strength to overcome challenges. Inspired by this message, Jennie-Lou deepened her faith and actively engaged with her spirituality, finding solace and support through prayer and meditation.

As Jennie-Lou continued acknowledging her feelings and confronting her self-doubt, her mindset shifted. Her resilience, determination, newfound confidence, and self-assurance unlocked her true potential.

Jennie-Lou's remarkable transformation proves the incredible impact of self-awareness, perseverance, and steadfast belief in one's potential. Through personal growth, she became more open, vulnerable, and accepting of herself and her emotions.

One critical insight Jennie-Lou gained was the importance of opening up and sharing her struggles with others. She reinforced her negative self-image by keeping her feelings and self-doubt bottled up. Jennie-Lou realized she needed to share her experiences and create a supportive network to heal and move forward.

Sharing her story with friends, family, and strangers, Jennie-Lou found many who could relate and offered valuable perspectives and advice. This connection and support helped her feel less isolated on her journey of self-discovery and growth, providing the encouragement she needed.

Over time, Jennie-Lou's commitment to acknowledging her feelings and embracing self-doubt led her to develop a stronger, more resilient mindset. She found that confronting her fears and insecurities allowed her to overcome them and tap into her potential.

Jennie-Lou's journey shows the importance of acknowledging feelings and embracing self-doubt as vital steps in the journey towards personal growth and success. Doing this can break down barriers and forge a path towards a brighter, more fulfilling future.

As you follow Jennie-Lou's journey, let her experiences remind you that no matter how difficult the road ahead may seem, there's always a way to rise above and achieve the life you want. Be inspired to confront your self-doubt, embrace your emotions, and forge your path to success and happiness.

Remember, each of us has the power to overcome self-doubt and achieve greatness. We must harness this power, face our fears, and create the life we've always dreamed of.

Key takeaways:

1. Recognize and accept self-doubt: The first step in overcoming self-doubt is acknowledging its presence in your life and understanding that it is a natural human emotion experienced by everyone.

2. Journaling as a tool for processing emotions: Journaling can help process emotions and gain insights into the root causes of self-doubt, allowing for personal growth and understanding.

3. Importance of faith and spirituality: Seeking solace and support through prayer, meditation, or engaging with one's spirituality can provide strength to overcome challenges and self-doubt.

4. Embracing emotions and self-doubt leads to personal growth: By facing fears and insecurities head-on, one can develop a stronger, more resilient mindset and unlock their true potential.

Action step:

Start a journaling practice: Set aside time each day to write about your feelings, fears, and insecurities. Use this practice to process your emotions, understand the root causes of your self-doubt, and identify areas for personal growth and improvement.

Reflection: Reflecting on your own experiences with self-doubt, can you identify any specific events, societal pressures, or past failures that have contributed to your feelings of self-doubt, and how can you use Jennie-Lou's story to inspire yourself to confront these feelings and work towards building a stronger, more resilient mindset?

CHAPTER 4

Identifying the Source of Her Doubt - The Quest for Self-Understanding and Divine Guidance

As Jennie-Lou continued her journey of self-discovery, she realized that to conquer her self-doubt truly, she needed to understand its origins. She knew that by identifying the source of her doubt, she could begin to dismantle the underlying beliefs and assumptions that fueled her insecurities and fears.

With relentless determination, Jennie-Lou embarked on a quest for self-understanding. She looked into her past, examining her life experiences and reflecting on the moments and circumstances that had contributed to her feelings of doubt and insecurity. Through this reflective process, Jennie-Lou identified several key factors that had shaped her self-perception and added to her self-doubt, including her upbringing, societal expectations, and past failures.

Jennie-Lou understood that her upbringing had a significant impact on her self-doubt. As a child, she was often compared to her siblings and peers, which led her to question her worth and abilities. This constant comparison started a pattern of self-doubt that stayed with her into adulthood.

In addition to her upbringing, Jennie-Lou recognized that societal expectations had also played a role in fostering her self-doubt. The pressure to conform to specific standards and ideals—whether in terms of beauty, career success, or relationships—caused her to doubt her path and choices. She began to see that her self-doubt was primarily due to trying to fit into a mold not meant for her.

As Jennie-Lou gained insight into the roots of her self-doubt, she also turned to her faith for guidance and support. She found solace in the words of the Bible, which provided her with a framework for understanding her struggles and overcoming her fears. One passage that resonated deeply with Jennie-Lou was Romans 12:2, which reads, "Do not conform to the pattern of this world, but be transformed by the renewing of your mind. Then you will be able to test and approve what God's will is—his good, pleasing and perfect will." This verse reminded Jennie-Lou that her journey of self-discovery and transformation was a personal and spiritual endeavor, inextricably linked to her relationship with God and her pursuit of His divine will.

Another verse that encouraged Jennie-Lou was 2 Timothy 1:7, which states, "For God has not given us a spirit of fear, but of power and of love and of a sound mind." This scripture reinforced that self-doubt and fear were not part of God's plan for her life. Instead, she was meant to embrace her inherent power, love, and wisdom.

Jennie-Lou realized the flaws in her past beliefs and assumptions as she reflected on biblical teachings and her understanding of her self-doubt's sources. She realized that much of her doubt was rooted in a desire to conform to the expectations of others and the world around her, rather than pursuing her unique path and God-given purpose.

Inspired by her faith and the wisdom of Scripture, Jennie-Lou resolved to renew her mind and transform her thinking in alignment with God's will for her life. She sought to replace her old, limiting beliefs with a new set of empowering convictions grounded in the truth of her divine identity and potential.

Jennie-Lou also committed to journaling her thoughts, emotions, and action steps throughout her transformation journey. This practice allowed her to document her progress and provided her with a valuable resource to reflect on when faced with future challenges or self-doubt. Moreover, she hoped her journal could inspire and guide others struggling with similar issues.

In this riveting chapter of Jennie-Lou's story, we witness the power of self-reflection and faith in transforming her life. As she uncovered the roots of her self-doubt and followed God's plan, she strengthened her resolve to overcome her insecurities. She started building the foundation for her future success.

As she continued to journal her experiences, Jennie-Lou found that this practice helped her process her thoughts and emotions and allowed her to celebrate her progress and growth. With each entry, she better understood her journey and the invaluable lessons she was learning.

Jennie-Lou's transformation was visible not only to herself but also to those around her. Her newfound confidence and determination attracted like-minded individuals who supported and encouraged her to pursue greatness. These relationships were a vital source of inspiration and motivation, helping Jennie-Lou remain steadfast in her journey, despite the problems and challenges she faced.

Key takeaways:

1. Introspection and understanding the origins of self-doubt: Reflecting on past experiences, upbringing, and societal expectations can help identify the factors contributing to self-doubt, allowing for personal growth.

2. Renewing the mind and aligning with one's purpose: Replacing limiting beliefs with empowering convictions grounded in one's divine identity and potential can lead to personal transformation and alignment with one's purpose.

3. Journaling as a tool for tracking progress and growth: Documenting thoughts, emotions, and action steps can help process experiences, celebrate progress, and serve as a resource for reflection and inspiration.

4. Building supportive relationships: Connecting with like-minded individuals who encourage and support personal growth can help maintain motivation and perseverance in the face of setbacks and challenges.

Action step:

Reflect on the origins of your self-doubt: Set aside time for introspection and self-examination, considering how your upbringing, past experiences, and societal expectations may have contributed to your self-doubt. Understanding these factors will help you address the root causes and work towards overcoming your insecurities.

Reflection: Reflect on your own life and consider the sources of your self-doubt. How has your upbringing, societal expectations, or past failures affected your insecurities? Using Jennie-Lou's journey as an example, what steps can you take to better understand and overcome your self-doubt and align with your unique path and purpose?

CHAPTER 5

The Power of Self-Compassion - Cultivating Kindness Within

In the early stages of her journey, Jennie-Lou's self-doubt often left her feeling defeated and unworthy of success. She was hard on herself, focusing on her perceived shortcomings and allowing her negative thoughts to consume her. One thought that kept coming back was her belief that she was a failure because she had not attained a prestigious job title. This thought often sent her spiraling into bouts of anxiety and sadness. It was not until she discovered the power of self-compassion that she began to break free from the shackles of self-doubt and embrace her true potential.

As Jennie-Lou continued her journey, she came across teachings about self-compassion. These teachings highlighted the importance of treating yourself with kindness, understanding, and love. Intrigued by this concept, she decided to delve deeper, exploring books, articles, and online resources to gain a deeper understanding of the principles and techniques of self-compassion. She took a particular interest in the work of Dr. Kristin Neff, a leading expert in the field. She found her book "Self-Compassion: The Proven Power of Being Kind to Yourself" enlightening. She attended workshops and seminars, looking for advice from experts to improve her knowledge and skills.

One of the key components of self-compassion that resonated with Jennie-Lou was the idea of treating oneself as a loving friend or family member. She began to reflect on the countless times she had offered others support, encouragement, and understanding, only to deny herself the same kindness. This realization was a turning point for Jennie-Lou, a moment of profound insight that would forever change the direction of her journey.

This sparked a transformation that was far from instantaneous. Jennie-Lou had days where she fell back into her old habit of self-criticism, but she learned to acknowledge these setbacks as part of the process. Each moment of self-doubt became an opportunity to practice self-compassion.

With a renewed sense of purpose, Jennie-Lou cultivated the practice of self-compassion daily. She started by addressing her inner critic, challenging the negative thoughts and beliefs that fueled her self-doubt. In one instance, she caught herself spiraling into feelings of inadequacy after a minor mistake at work. Instead of succumbing to these feelings, she consciously replaced her negative thoughts with words of kindness and encouragement, telling herself, "It's okay to make mistakes. You're still learning and growing." Each time a self-deprecating thought arose, she would consciously replace it with words of kindness and encouragement, reminding herself of her inherent worth and her progress. She also developed a daily self-compassion practice, setting aside time daily to meditate, reflect on her accomplishments, and express gratitude for her many blessings.

In addition to silencing her inner critic, Jennie-Lou learned to forgive herself for past mistakes and perceived failures. When she recalled her unsuccessful attempt to start a business years ago, instead of letting it weigh her down, she reframed it as a valuable learning experience that taught her about resilience and adaptability. She acknowledged that everyone, even the most successful, faced setbacks and made mistakes. This realization allowed her to view her experiences not as failures but as valuable learning opportunities that contributed to her personal growth and development. Through practicing self-compassion, Jennie-Lou started to appreciate the wisdom she gained from her past experiences, viewing them as stepping stones to her future success.

As Jennie-Lou deepened her practice of self-compassion, she began to undergo a profound transformation. Her self-doubt slowly faded, replaced by a growing sense of confidence and self-assurance. She set a goal to start a new project at work, something she had been too afraid to take on in the past. Equipped with her newfound self-belief, she was ready to challenge herself, and she was amazed at the results. She found herself better prepared to face life's challenges, embracing each new experience with courage and resilience. Jennie-Lou also started setting more ambitious goals for herself, confident in her ability to overcome any obstacles that stood in her way.

As her self-compassion practice grew, so did her ability to set and maintain healthy boundaries. She understood that this was not selfish but necessary for her own well-being. She acknowledged that she couldn't always make everyone happy, but that was okay. Her focus was on earning respect rather than just being liked. She learned This lesson from a business coach, who asked her an important question: "Would you rather be liked or respected?"

Jennie-Lou's journey was not without challenges, but her newfound practice of self-compassion and self-care was transformative. It allowed her to grow as a person and find a sense of purpose and direction in her life. A pivotal moment in her journey was when she heard the song "I'm Moving On" by Rascal Flatts. The lyrics struck a chord with her, especially "I've lived in this place and I know all the faces each one is different, but they're always the same." This song spoke to her about the importance of moving beyond the expectations and constraints of others to truly become who she is meant to be.

As Martin Luther King Jr. once said, "The measure of a man is not where he stands in moments of comfort and convenience, but where he stands at times of challenge and controversy." Jennie-Lou found this quote to be particularly relevant in her journey of self-discovery. She began to recognize that her worth was not tied to her job title or other external markers of success but rather to the content of her character.

Through the continuous process of growth and development, she began to value herself for who she was, to focus on her own personal growth and self-discovery, and not let the opinions of others define her. She learned to go easier on herself and found the strength to accept her past and move on from it. She made a conscious choice to show up for herself every day. It was not always easy, but it was the best decision she had ever made.

Jennie-Lou also noticed that her newfound self-compassion had a ripple effect, positively impacting her relationships with others. As she became kinder and more understanding toward herself, she found it easier to extend the same compassion to those around her. This shift improved her relationships and strengthened her support network, providing her with valuable encouragement and camaraderie in her journey.

The practice of self-compassion played a crucial role in Jennie-Lou's transformation, allowing her to overcome her self-doubt and step into her power. Through kindness, understanding, and forgiveness, she was able to silence her inner critic, embrace her strengths, and build a solid foundation for future success.

As Jennie-Lou's journey unfolded, she discovered that self-compassion was not a destination but a lifelong practice that required ongoing commitment and effort. By continually nurturing her self-compassion, she was able to weather the storms of life and emerge stronger, more resilient, and ready to conquer any challenge that came her way.

Jennie-Lou found solace in the Bible's words, which gave her the strength to persevere in her self-compassion journey. A particular verse that resonated with her was Philippians 4:13, which states, "I can do all things through

Christ who strengthens me." This verse reminded Jennie-Lou that she was never alone in her journey and that a higher power was always by her side, guiding her and providing her with the strength to overcome her challenges.

As time passed, Jennie-Lou's practice of self-compassion continued to grow and strengthen, becoming a crucial part of her everyday life. She found that the more she fostered this self-compassion, the more resilient, confident, and empowered she felt.

Jennie-Lou's journey stands as a potent testament to the transformative power of self-compassion. By learning to extend the same kindness, understanding, and love she offered others to herself, she overcame her self-doubt and achieved her dreams.

Through her story, Jennie-Lou shares a valuable lesson: that cultivating self-compassion can not only help us conquer self-doubt, but also unlock our true potential and build a life filled with happiness, fulfillment, and success. May Jennie-Lou's journey inspire you to adopt the practice of self-compassion and discover the boundless possibilities within you.

Key takeaways

1. Resilience is key to overcoming setbacks: Building resilience allows individuals to face obstacles and setbacks with greater confidence and determination, ultimately helping them achieve their goals and dreams.

2. Mindset shift: Cultivating resilience involves shifting one's mindset to view challenges as growth opportunities rather than insurmountable barriers. This shift enables individuals to learn from their experiences and develop their skills and abilities.

3. Embracing failure: One aspect of building resilience is accepting and embracing failure as a natural part of the learning process. By treating failures as valuable lessons, individuals can grow from their mistakes and develop the perseverance required to achieve long-term success.

4. Self-care and stress management: Practicing self-care and effective stress management techniques is crucial for maintaining resilience in the face of adversity. You can better handle stress and maintain your motivation and focus by prioritizing physical, emotional, and mental well-being.

Action steps

1. Adopt a growth mindset: Practice viewing challenges as opportunities for learning and growth. When faced with

obstacles or setbacks, reflect on the lessons they offer and how you can apply this knowledge to improve your skills and abilities in the future.

2. Prioritize self-care and stress management: Schedule regular self-care activities, such as exercise, meditation, or hobbies, to maintain your well-being and reduce stress. Implement stress management techniques, like deep breathing exercises or mindfulness practices, to help you stay focused and resilient in the face of challenges.

Reflection: Reflect on your self-compassion practices and how you treat yourself when faced with setbacks or perceived failures. How can you implement self-compassion techniques in your daily life to silence your inner critic, foster resilience, and strengthen your confidence?

Chapter 6

The Power of Celebrating Successes - Recognizing Every Victory, Big or Small

Jennie-Lou had a habit of dwelling on her failures, a tendency that only fueled her self-doubt. Yet, she was resolute in escaping this harmful cycle. One strategy she adopted was to celebrate her victories, regardless of how minor they seemed.

This decision was born out of a late-night introspective moment. Sitting in her dimly lit room, enveloped by the quiet ticking of the clock, she experienced a sudden revelation: her self-doubt didn't stem from an actual lack of ability or value but rather her propensity to focus on failures instead of triumphs.

She started by maintaining a journal to record her accomplishments. Each day, she would write down at least one thing she had accomplished, whether it was completing a difficult task at work, making a healthy choice for dinner, or simply managing to keep her anxiety under control. Over time, this practice helped Jennie-Lou shift her perspective and focus on the positive aspects of her life.

As she filled up her journal, she started including reflections with each entry, probing deeper into what each success meant to her. She not only listed her accomplishments but also expressed the feelings they evoked and the insights they provided. This practice of deeper reflection enabled her to appreciate her growth in a more meaningful way.

As her journal became filled with small and big wins, Jennie-Lou's confidence and belief in herself grew stronger. She began to realize that she wasn't the failure her self-doubt had made her believe. Instead, she was a powerful, resilient woman who was making consistent progress, one step at a time.

This newfound perspective improved Jennie-Lou's outlook on life and significantly impacted her relationships with others. Her friends and family noticed a change in her demeanor as she became more optimistic and self-assured. Her determination and growth inspired them; some even adopted similar practices to overcome self-doubt.

This transformation was noticed by Jennie-Lou. She observed how her positivity was creating a ripple effect, inspiring her loved ones to tackle their self-doubt. This observation deepened her commitment to her journey of self-improvement.

Jennie-Lou realized that celebrating her successes built her confidence and inspired those around her. This powerful realization motivated her to continue pushing forward, even in the face of adversity.

She created a new narrative with each documented accomplishment recognizing her strength, resilience, and determination. She began to embrace the idea that every success, no matter how seemingly insignificant, was a victory worth celebrating. In celebrating this victory, Jennie-Lou treated herself to a nice dinner in a restaurant she had always wanted to visit. During her dinner, she thought to herself, "Why don't I purchase a bracelet to act as a reminder of my success." She then went to a jewelry store and purchased herself a beautiful bracelet to remind her of her journey.

The bracelet was a symbol of her strength, a constant reminder of the journey she had embarked on. Each time she glanced at it, she was reminded of the progress she had made, and it spurred her on to continue pursuing her goals.

Jennie-Lou's journal became a testament to her transformation as the months passed. She would often flip through the pages, reflecting on the challenges she had overcome and the progress she had made. It was a tangible reminder of her journey and a source of inspiration whenever self-doubt returned.

By choosing to celebrate her successes, Jennie-Lou could rewrite her story and redefine her identity. She proved to herself that she was capable of greatness and, in doing so, unlocked the door to a brighter, more fulfilling future.

One evening, as Jennie-Lou sat down to reflect on her journey, she realized that her newly found ability to acknowledge and celebrate her victories had not just transformed her life but also set her on a path toward helping others. She was a woman who had learned to value herself, who had come to understand that her worth was not determined by her failures but by her strength and resilience in the face of adversity. She felt profoundly grateful for the lessons she had learned and knew that it was her responsibility to share her experiences with those who might be struggling with self-doubt, as she had once had.

Jennie-Lou's celebration of her victories and the sharing of her journey became a beacon of hope and inspiration for others. Her dedication to acknowledging the beauty in every triumph, no matter how small, deeply resonated with those who heard her story. Through her example, they began to realize that surmounting self-doubt and achieving their dreams was possible, even amidst adversity.

While documenting her successes, Jennie-Lou also recognized patterns and trends in her personal growth. She discovered that specific actions, habits, and mindsets were more likely to lead to positive outcomes. Consequently, she became increasingly intentional about incorporating these practices into her daily life. She came to appreciate the power of music in her life. The song "I'm Moving On" marked a turning point for her, motivating her to confront her own insecurities and strive for personal growth and fulfillment. Although the journey was challenging, it was pivotal for her mental and emotional well-being. The song resonated with her, reminding her it was acceptable to distance herself from individuals who limited her, even if unintentionally. It encouraged her to foster her self-esteem and be proud of who she was and what she had accomplished.

This intentional focus on personal development not only helped Jennie-Lou to achieve her goals but also allowed her to inspire others who were struggling with self-doubt. By sharing her story and the lessons she had learned along the way, Jennie-Lou became a powerful catalyst for change in the lives of those around her. With a heart full of compassion and a desire to uplift others, she embarked on a mission to directly help those who were facing similar struggles. Jennie-Lou knew that by sharing her experiences, she could inspire and empower others to overcome self-doubt and take control of their lives.

Jennie-Lou engaged with individuals from all walks of life through speaking engagements, workshops, and online platforms, creating a safe space for open dialogue and heartfelt connections. Her friendly and conversational approach allowed others to relate to her experiences, making her an approachable and relatable mentor.

During these sessions, Jennie-Lou shared the transformative power of faith, positivity, and personal development. She emphasized the importance of trusting in God's plan, embracing a positive mindset, and investing in oneself. Jennie-Lou passionately encouraged her listeners to challenge their limiting beliefs, redefine their self-worth, and embrace the incredible potential within them.

But Jennie-Lou's impact extended far beyond words and inspiration. She looked back on what helped her overcome her struggles and realized that having a coach and mentor was instrumental to her growth and success. She took it upon herself to provide practical guidance and support to those who sought her guidance. Through personalized coaching and mentorship programs, she guided individuals step by step, helping them develop strategies tailored to their unique circumstances and aspirations. Whether it was overcoming financial hurdles, setting ambitious goals, or embarking on new career paths, Jennie-Lou was there as a steadfast ally, supporting others on their journey to success.

Jennie-Lou's genuine desire to help others and her own success story created a ripple effect of transformation. Those who had once felt stuck in the depths of self-doubt and despair found renewed hope and a sense of possibility. They embraced Jennie-Lou's shared principles and took decisive action to turn their lives around.

Through her unwavering dedication to serving others, Jennie-Lou witnessed countless individuals rediscovering their self-belief, reclaiming their dreams, and experiencing breakthroughs that surpassed their expectations. She celebrated each success story as a testament to the transformative power of faith, positivity, and personal development.

With every success she celebrated and every person she helped, Jennie-Lou's sense of purpose and fulfillment grew stronger. She began to understand that her journey, while marked by pain and struggle, was ultimately a testament to the power of resilience and self-belief.

As Jennie-Lou's story continues to unfold, it serves as a potent reminder that our lives are shaped by the stories we tell ourselves. By acknowledging and celebrating our successes, we can rewrite our narratives and create a future filled with hope, resilience, and self-belief.

Key takeaways

1. Focus on achievements: Shifting focus from failures to achievements helps build self-confidence and overcome self-doubt.

2. Document accomplishments: Keeping a journal to document daily accomplishments, no matter how small, can help reinforce self-belief and maintain a positive outlook on life.

3. Celebrating successes inspires others: Celebrating one's achievements can inspire others to adopt similar practices and work towards overcoming self-doubt.

4. Recognize personal growth patterns: Being intentional about incorporating positive actions, habits, and mindsets can lead to better outcomes and personal development.

5. Embrace the power of self-belief: By acknowledging and honoring achievements, one can create a future filled with hope, happiness, and the freedom to pursue dreams, irrespective of their size.

Action step

Reflect on and learn from your experiences: Regularly review your journal entries and accomplishments to identify patterns, habits, and mindsets contributing to your growth. Use this insight to intentionally incorporate these positive practices into your daily life, fostering resilience and self-belief.

Reflection: Reflect on your own experiences and consider the successes, big or small, that you may have overlooked or downplayed in your life. How can you begin to acknowledge and celebrate these accomplishments to shift your focus from self-doubt to self-belief and foster personal growth?

CHAPTER 7

Unleashing Faith - Jennie-Lou's Journey to Conquer Self-Doubt

In the midst of her struggles, Jennie-Lou sought guidance and support in her faith. She found comfort in biblical teachings, and her spiritual journey became a critical component of her path towards overcoming self-doubt.

As she delved deeper into her faith, Jennie-Lou began attending regular worship services, soaking up the wisdom of scripture. She found inspiration in stories of individuals who had, against all odds, triumphed over adversity through their steadfast faith in a higher power. One biblical passage that particularly resonated with her was Philippians 4:13, which states, 'I can do all things through Christ who strengthens me.' This verse became a constant source of comfort and empowerment for Jennie-Lou, reminding her that she was never alone in her struggles.

With every sermon she heard and page she read, Jennie-Lou embraced the notion that she could overcome her challenges if she trusted in God. This belief laid the foundation for her new life, and this faith helped her remain strong in the face of uncertainty and fear.

As Jennie-Lou deepened her spiritual practice, she discovered that prayer and meditation were potent tools for combating self-doubt. Through these practices, she learned to quiet her mind and find peace in the midst of her tumultuous thoughts. She recognized the power of surrender, releasing her fears and anxieties to a higher power and allowing divine wisdom to guide her.

In her quiet moments of reflection, Jennie-Lou also began to understand the importance of gratitude. She realized that by focusing on the blessings in her life, she could counteract the negative thoughts and feelings that fed her self-doubt. Each day, she made a conscious effort to express gratitude for the opportunities she had been given, the people who supported her, and her progress. She took inspiration from 1 Thessalonians 5:18, which encourages us to "give thanks in all circumstances; for this is the will of God in Christ Jesus for you."

As Jennie-Lou nurtured an attitude of gratitude, her perspective began to shift. She found herself more attuned to the good in her life, even amidst the struggles. This change in her mindset also positively affected her relationships, fostering a deeper sense of connection and understanding with those around her.

The impact of Jennie-Lou's faith extended beyond her personal life as she began to see the power of faith in the lives of those around her. She witnessed friends and family members overcoming their struggles through the strength they derived from their beliefs. Inspired by their stories, Jennie-Lou felt even more committed to her spiritual journey and the transformative power of faith.

One person who inspired her was a close friend who, despite battling a chronic illness, found strength and comfort in her faith. Watching her friend navigate her challenges with grace and resilience deepened Jennie-Lou's appreciation for the power of faith and its potential to foster inner strength and resilience.

Throughout Jennie-Lou's journey, we learn that faith overcomes self-doubt and catalyzes positive change in our lives. It provides the strength, courage, and perseverance to face our fears and create a brighter future for ourselves and others.

Jennie-Lou's spiritual journey helped her conquer self-doubt and taught her valuable lessons about resilience, determination, and maintaining a strong connection with her faith. Her story serves as a powerful testament to the transformative power of faith, reminding us all that we are capable of overcoming our challenges when we trust in a higher power and stay true to our beliefs. These experiences shaped her into the person she was meant to be, enabling her to pursue her dreams and succeed.

Key takeaways

1. Spiritual beliefs can provide guidance and support: Jennie-Lou found solace in her faith, which helped her overcome self-doubt and build a strong foundation for personal growth.

2. Prayer and meditation can be powerful tools for combating self-doubt: Through these practices, Jennie-Lou learned to quiet her mind, find peace amidst her thoughts, and surrender her fears and anxieties to a higher power.

3. Gratitude plays a significant role in shifting focus: By consciously expressing gratitude daily, Jennie-Lou counteracted the negative thoughts and feelings that fed her self-doubt and created a more positive outlook by consciously expressing gratitude daily.

Action step

Develop a daily prayer or meditation practice: Set aside time each day to focus on calming your mind and releasing fears and anxieties to a higher power or your inner wisdom.

Reflection: Reflect on the role of faith, spirituality, or a belief in something greater than yourself in your own life. How has this influenced your ability to overcome self-doubt and foster personal growth? If you have yet to explore this aspect of your life, how might doing so help you in your journey towards self-improvement and fulfillment?

CHAPTER 8

Taking Action - Small Steps to Overcoming Self-Doubt and Achieving Greatness

Amid her newfound confidence, Jennie-Lou acknowledged that it was vital to maintain a balance between dreaming big and taking practical steps to achieve her goals. She understood the importance of breaking her dreams into smaller, actionable steps that would gradually lead her to success. The journey toward greatness would be challenging, but she was determined to face every challenge with courage and resilience.

One evening, she sat at her desk, facing a blank notebook. With a determined spirit, she began to write, converting her dreams into Specific, Measurable, Achievable, Relevant, Time-bound, Evaluated, and Reviewed (SMARTER) goals. Jennie-Lou used the SMARTER goal-setting framework to ensure her goals were realistic and achievable. This approach provided her with clear objectives and a structured timeline to work towards, enabling her to focus her efforts and maintain her momentum throughout her journey.

She diligently created a detailed plan that outlined the specific steps she needed to take to make her dreams a reality. The task was daunting, but she tackled it with determination. This plan served as her roadmap, guiding her through her journey's ups and downs and helping her stay focused on her goals. She reviewed her plan and evaluated her progress daily, ensuring she stayed committed and accountable to her SMARTER goals.

To boost her chances of success, Jennie-Lou adopted a growth mindset. This mindset allowed her to view challenges as opportunities to learn and acquire new skills. It enabled her to see failure as an essential part of the journey, not as a crippling setback. One morning, as she made her usual cup of coffee, doubts began to seep in. But, reminding herself of her commitment to her growth mindset, she took a deep breath and decided to face the day with courage. As a result, she found herself more willing to take risks and venture outside her comfort zone, knowing that each new experience would contribute to her growth and progress.

Another critical aspect of Jennie-Lou's journey toward greatness was cultivating a strong support system. She surrounded herself with positive, like-minded individuals who shared her aspirations and values. Among them were her best friend, Maria, a constant source of encouragement and positivity, and John, a seasoned entrepreneur who provided invaluable advice from his own experiences. These connections gave her camaraderie and a safe space to discuss her struggles and celebrate her victories. By maintaining these relationships, Jennie-Lou found encouragement and inspiration that kept her moving forward, even when the going got tough.

In her quest for greatness, Jennie-Lou also discovered the importance of self-care and maintaining a healthy work-life balance. She realized she needed to take care of her physical, mental, and emotional well-being to achieve her SMARTER goals. She made it a point to incorporate regular exercise, a nutritious diet, and time for relaxation and self-reflection into her daily routine, knowing that this would help her maintain her energy levels and stay motivated.

As the weeks and months passed, Jennie-Lou began to see the fruits of her labor. Her small, consistent actions had laid the foundation for significant achievements, and she found herself closer to her goals than ever before. Her progress in meeting her SMARTER goals further fueled her determination and drive, giving her the confidence to take on even more significant challenges and strive for greatness.

Jennie-Lou's remarkable journey embodies the profound impact of taking decisive action and the significance of embarking on small, purposeful steps. As her story unfolds, it is a powerful reminder that even the loftiest aspirations can be realized through unwavering dedication, resilience in the face of adversity, and unshakeable self-belief. Her transformative experience echoes the wise words of Robert Collier, who once said, "Success is the sum of small efforts, repeated day in and day out."

Let Jennie-Lou's story inspire and guide you as you embark on your path toward greatness. Remember that every step, no matter how small, brings you closer to your dreams. By embracing a growth mindset, cultivating a solid support system, and setting SMARTER goals, you can overcome self-doubt and achieve the greatness you were always destined for. Her transformative experience is an inspiration to all who are daring to dream and willing to put in the work required to turn their dreams into reality.

key takeaways

1. Use the SMARTER goal-setting framework: Set Specific, Measurable, Achievable, Relevant, Time-bound, Evaluated, and Reviewed goals to provide clear objectives and a structured timeline for your journey toward success.

2. Develop a growth mindset: Embrace challenges as opportunities to learn and develop new skills, and view failure as an essential part of the journey, not a devastating setback.

3. Build a strong support system: Surround yourself with positive, like-minded individuals who share your aspirations and values, encouraging you to keep moving forward.

4. Prioritize self-care and work-life balance: Take care of your physical, mental, and emotional well-being through regular exercise, a nutritious diet, and time for relaxation and self-reflection to maintain energy levels and motivation.

5. Consistency is key: Focus on taking small, manageable steps consistently to lay the foundation for significant achievements and progress towards your goals.

Action steps

1. Create a detailed plan: Outline the specific steps you need to take to achieve your goals, using this plan as your roadmap

to guide you through your journey and help you stay focused on your objectives.

2. Review and assess progress regularly: Dedicate time each day or week to review your plan and evaluate your progress, ensuring that you remain accountable and committed to your SMARTER goals.

3. Take calculated risks: Push yourself beyond your comfort zone by taking risks that contribute to your growth and progress while learning from setbacks and using them as opportunities for improvement.

Reflection: Reflect on the goals you have set for yourself and consider whether they follow the SMARTER goal-setting framework. How can breaking down your goals into smaller, actionable steps help you overcome self-doubt and contribute to your personal growth? In what areas of your life can you apply a growth mindset to help you face challenges and learn from failures?

CHAPTER 9

Embracing Accountability - The Power of Mentoring and Personal Growth

As Jennie-Lou moved forward, she understood the value of seeking advice and support from others who had experienced similar journeys. She often found comfort in the words of Tony Robbins: "The power of coaching is this - you get to benefit from someone who's been where you've been, who is dedicated to your growth, and who will hold you accountable to reach what you truly desire." Despite her growing confidence, she realized that she still had much to learn and that having a coach could offer her invaluable insights and mentorship. Jennie-Lou was aware that accepting accountability and investing in personal growth could accelerate her path to success and help her unlock her full potential.

Jennie-Lou diligently searched for the perfect coach, eager to find someone who would hold her accountable and ignite her inner fire for growth. She attended countless seminars, conferences, and networking events, hoping to find the right mentor to guide her along her journey.

It was at an entrepreneurial summit, where Jennie-Lou least expected it, that she found herself seated next to a charismatic individual named Jacques. Engaging in conversation, they quickly discovered their shared passion for personal development and desire to make a significant impact.

As the event progressed, Jennie-Lou couldn't help but notice Jacques's unwavering energy and enthusiasm. In a casual conversation during a break, Jacques mentioned the life-changing impact of "The 5 AM Club" by Robin Sharma. Intrigued, Jennie-Lou immediately sensed a deep connection with Jacques and her words, feeling that this encounter was destined.

Driven by curiosity and a yearning for growth, Jennie-Lou delved into "The 5 AM Club" and discovered a wealth of wisdom within its pages. Inspired by the book's powerful concepts on mindset, peak performance, and personal mastery, she realized she had found a coach and a kindred spirit in Jacques.

Jennie-Lou took the leap of faith and approached Jacques, expressing her desire to be mentored. Their shared values and goals created an instant bond, and Jacques gladly accepted the opportunity to guide Jennie-Lou on her transformative journey.

With Jacques's guidance, Jennie-Lou's growth accelerated exponentially. Their coaching sessions became powerful catalysts for self-discovery and breakthroughs. Jacques's wealth of experience and expertise allowed her to offer invaluable insights, guiding Jennie-Lou through the challenges and empowering her to push beyond her perceived limits.

Jennie-Lou was grateful for the trust and rapport that developed between her and Jacques. It was a partnership built on mutual respect, understanding, and a shared commitment to unleashing Jennie-Lou's full potential. Jacques's unwavering support and belief in Jennie-Lou's capabilities became the fuel that propelled her forward, even during the most challenging moments.

Together, Jennie-Lou and Jacques worked diligently, navigating the ups and downs of her entrepreneurial journey. Through Jacques's guidance, Jennie-Lou cultivated an unwavering resilience, a laser-focused mindset, and an unshakeable belief in her abilities.

Jennie-Lou and Jacques developed a personalized coaching plan tailored to Jennie-Lou's needs and objectives. They established specific milestones and regularly scheduled check-ins to assess her progress, ensuring she remained on track and accountable for her actions. They made sure that each session was an opportunity for growth and learning, focusing on refining strategies, honing skills, and furthering Jennie-Lou's understanding of her motivations and capabilities. Through these sessions, Jennie-Lou received invaluable feedback, encouragement, and advice, enabling her to refine her approach and overcome any barriers that arose.

During the coaching process, Jennie-Lou discovered the transformative power of reflection and introspection. She learned to objectively analyze her thoughts, beliefs, and actions to identify areas for improvement and growth. She began to see her life from a different perspective, understanding that her actions today would shape her tomorrow. This realization was pivotal, prompting her to continually strive for self-improvement and growth. By engaging in this process, Jennie-Lou was able to develop a deeper understanding of herself and gain clarity on her goals and aspirations.

As their coaching relationship flourished, Jennie-Lou's life began to transform in remarkable ways. She achieved breakthroughs she had once deemed impossible, conquered her self-doubt, and emerged as a confident and purpose-driven individual ready to leave her mark on the world.

Jennie-Lou's unexpected encounter with Jacques had become a turning point in her life. The connection they formed and the guidance she received enabled Jennie-Lou to tap into her untapped potential, propelling her towards extraordinary achievements she had never thought possible.

One of Jennie-Lou's most important lessons from her coaching experience was the power of resilience and perseverance. Through the guidance of her coach, she discovered that setbacks were inevitable, but they could be used as opportunities for growth and learning. She learned to embrace failure as a natural part of the process and use it to fuel her determination to succeed. She began to view challenges not as roadblocks, but as stepping stones towards her dreams.

As Jennie-Lou and Jacques continued working together, they delved deeper into her fears and insecurities. They identified her limiting beliefs and worked on replacing them with empowering thoughts and affirmations. This process helped Jennie-Lou to develop a more positive mindset and foster stronger confidence in her abilities.

The coaching relationship also helped Jennie-Lou recognize the value of self-compassion. As Jennie-Lou nurtured her self-compassion, she found it easier to recover from setbacks and stay motivated, even in tough times. She learned to be gentle and understanding with herself, recognizing that self-doubt and obstacles are just normal parts of the journey.

One unique aspect of Jennie-Lou's coaching experience was the emphasis on creating a supportive network. Jacques, her coach, urged her to connect with others who shared her goals and aspirations. This circle of like-minded peers gave Jennie-Lou extra encouragement, advice, and a sense of camaraderie, further strengthening her resolve to succeed.

In the end, Jacques' coaching played a critical role in Jennie-Lou's journey to personal growth. The coaching experience equipped her with the tools, guidance, and support she needed to overcome self-doubt and tackle the challenges of chasing her dreams. By accepting accountability and investing in personal growth, Jennie-Lou managed to lay a robust foundation for success and unlock her full potential.

key takeaways

1. Importance of Coaching: Jennie-Lou realized the value of partnering with a coach to provide her invaluable insights, support, and accountability in her personal growth and success journey.

2. Embracing accountability and personal growth: By working with a coach, Jennie-Lou committed to a personalized coaching plan and engaged in regular check-ins, which helped her stay on track and accountable for her progress.

3. Power of reflection and introspection: Through the coaching process, Jennie-Lou learned to objectively analyze her thoughts, beliefs, and actions to identify areas for improvement, gain clarity on her goals, and develop a deeper understanding of herself.

4. Developing resilience, perseverance, and self-compassion: Jennie-Lou's coaching experience taught her the importance of embracing setbacks as opportunities for growth and learning, cultivating self-compassion, and maintaining motivation in the face of adversity.

Action steps

Find a coach or mentor: Find an experienced coach or mentor who aligns with your values and can provide guidance, support, and accountability in your journey towards personal growth and achieving your goals. Interview potential candidates to ensure a strong rapport and trust.

Reflection: Reflect on your journey and consider the areas where you could benefit from guidance or mentorship. How might embracing accountability and seeking support from a coach or mentor help you overcome self-doubt and achieve your goals? How can you develop a support network of like-minded individuals to encourage and inspire you along your path to personal growth and success?

Part III: Pursuing Her Dreams

CHAPTER 10

A Bold Leap - The Emotional Rollercoaster of Jennie-Lou's First Attempt at Real Estate

Jennie-Lou's transformative journey of self-discovery and personal growth had laid a strong emotional foundation, empowering her to take a bold leap towards her real estate dreams. Fueled by her newfound confidence and unwavering determination, she pursued her passion for property investment, eager to make a positive impact in the industry.

Intrigued by the prospect of creating wealth through real estate, Jennie-Lou initially set her sights on the world of short-term rentals. She immersed herself in extensive research, tirelessly networking, and acquiring the knowledge necessary for success. This phase of her journey was not merely about gathering information; it became a humbling lesson in perseverance and patience. Jennie-Lou attended seminars, workshops, and real estate meetups, immersing herself in the wisdom of industry experts and forging valuable connections with fellow investors. With unwavering determination, she invested in courses and mentorship programs, determined to equip herself with the necessary tools for her new venture.

Despite her thorough preparations, managing short-term rentals proved to be more challenging than anticipated. While setbacks are an inevitable part of any journey, Jennie-Lou confronted an array of responsibilities. From marketing her properties and managing bookings to addressing guests' needs and maintaining her rental units, the demands seemed overwhelming.

As Jennie-Lou embarked on her real estate journey, she found herself on an emotional rollercoaster. Just as a mountain range presents both peaks and valleys, her experiences oscillated between exhilarating highs and daunting lows. The thrill of a fully booked property and the joy of satisfied guests fueled her motivation, reaffirming her belief that she was on the right path. However, these moments of triumph were often shadowed by the disheartening challenges of unexpected cancellations, maintenance issues, and problematic tenants.

At this critical juncture, Jennie-Lou faced a treacherous road with an unclear path ahead. The stress and uncertainty of her new venture took a toll on her initial enthusiasm. The weight of financial stability and the pressure to succeed burdened her shoulders. Doubt began to creep back into her thoughts, causing her to question the validity of her decision and her preparedness to overcome the industry's hurdles.

But Jennie-Lou's unwavering spirit and resilience shone through the darkness. She turned to her journal, not just as a medium for reflection but as a guiding light to navigate the storm. In revisiting her past entries and the action steps she had recorded, she drew strength from her own words and experiences. Jennie-Lou refused to let setbacks define her. Instead, she embraced them as opportunities for growth and learning. With each setback, she grew stronger, determined to rise above the challenges that came her way.

During this tumultuous period in her real estate journey, Jennie-Lou began to recognize a shift within herself. She realized that her true passion lay not in the volatile world of short-term rentals, but in the more stable and predictable realm of long-term rentals. Longer tenancies and a consistent income stream appealed to her innate desire for stability and sustainability. Jennie-Lou's ability to reflect on her experiences and adapt her strategy was a testament to her growth and newfound self-belief.

In the face of her short-term rental setbacks, Jennie-Lou found the resilience to pivot and redirect her efforts toward long-term rentals. With her determination as her compass, she meticulously analyzed market trends, carefully selected investment properties, and honed her property management skills. By embracing the stability and reliability of long-term rentals, Jennie-Lou discovered a new avenue to fulfill her passion and achieve her real estate aspirations.

Jennie-Lou's journey showcases the transformative power of resilience and adaptability. It is a reminder that setbacks are not the end, but catalysts for growth and redirection. By embracing the unexpected and pivoting when necessary, we can uncover new opportunities and forge a path towards success. Jennie-Lou's unwavering belief in herself and her ability to learn from her experiences serve as an inspiration for aspiring real estate entrepreneurs, highlighting the importance of perseverance, self-reflection, and the courage to pivot when faced with adversity.

As Jennie-Lou's journey unfolds, we bear witness to the transformative power of resilience and the unwavering pursuit of one's dreams. Her story, filled with both trials and triumphs, encourages us to navigate the rollercoaster of real estate with determination, adaptability, and the willingness to seize new opportunities, even when they present themselves in unexpected ways.

Key Insights:

1. Thorough preparation is crucial: Jennie-Lou dedicated significant time to researching, networking, and acquiring knowledge to succeed in her real estate venture. This helped her navigate the market's complexities and adapt her strategies when needed.

2. Emotional resilience is essential: The real estate journey brought numerous highs and lows, testing Jennie-Lou's emotional resilience. By remembering the lessons she learned on her journey to overcome self-doubt, she persevered and learned from her experiences.

3. Reflect on experiences and adapt: When Jennie-Lou realized her true passion lay elsewhere, she adapted her strategy and focused on mid-term rentals. This ability to reflect and pivot was vital to her growth and success in the industry.

4. Challenges provide growth opportunities: Jennie-Lou faced each challenge with grit and grace, understanding that every obstacle was an opportunity for growth and personal development. This mindset helped her to overcome self-doubt and embrace her true potential.

5. Share your story to inspire others: Jennie-Lou's journey led to her success and inspired others facing similar struggles. By

sharing her experiences and lessons, she encouraged others to believe in their potential and chase their dreams.

Action steps:

1. Cultivate emotional resilience: Practice maintaining a positive outlook and persevere even when facing setbacks. Develop coping strategies to handle stress and uncertainty, and remember that challenges can provide opportunities for growth and learning.

2. Regularly reflect and adapt: Periodically assess your progress, goals, and strategies. Be open to change and adapt your approach when necessary. Embrace flexibility and be willing to pivot when new opportunities or passions arise, ensuring you stay aligned with your true objectives and aspirations.

Reflection: Reflect on a challenging situation or decision you have faced in your own life. How did you overcome the emotional rollercoaster that accompanied this experience? What lessons did you learn from it, and how can you apply them to future challenges to maintain your confidence and resilience in the face of adversity?

Chapter 11

Resilience Awakened - Unveiling the Passion for Mid-Term Rentals on an Emotional Expedition

Jennie-Lou, a determined woman with an entrepreneurial spirit, was always fascinated by the world of real estate. Growing up in a small town, she admired the unique charm and potential each property possessed. This fascination, combined with her goal of achieving financial independence, led her to real estate investment.

Jennie-Lou's journey in real estate investment took an unexpected twist when her initial venture into short-term rentals didn't meet her expectations. However, she recognized that these setbacks were not the end of her journey but a chance to rethink her strategy and rekindle her true passion.

In a quiet moment of introspection, she recalled her first investment property and the thrill she had felt when she finalized the deal. It was a humble two-bedroom house that she had dreamt of converting into a vibrant short-term rental. Yet, the task of managing such a business turned out to be more complex and demanding than she had envisioned.

Alone in her home office, Jennie-Lou faced her unsuccessful investments, determined not to let them define her. She felt a whirlwind of emotions - frustration, self-doubt, hope, and determination. While frustration nagged her, self-doubt whispered uncertainties into her ear. However, hope persisted as a steadfast spark, refusing to be snuffed out. With her eyes still set on her ultimate goal of achieving financial freedom and making a positive impact, she looked for a new path.

She remembered the words of her grandmother, a woman of fierce resolve and resilience, "When one door closes, another opens. You just have to find the right key." Drawing strength from this wisdom, Jennie-Lou was determined to turn this setback into an opportunity.

For weeks, Jennie-Lou immersed herself in researching different real estate niches and strategies, seeking one that aligned with her values and passions. The mornings that were once filled with video games transformed into webinars, while evenings previously occupied by TV shows turned into online real estate forums. She eagerly attended seminars, joined discussions, and sought guidance from experienced investors. It was during one such conversation that she discovered the world of mid-term rentals.

One evening, while participating in an online forum, a seasoned investor named Robert mentioned the concept of mid-term rentals. Intrigued, Jennie-Lou reached out to him for further guidance. Their enlightening conversation sparked her interest in this untapped market, offering an alternative path to her short-term rental venture.

Intrigued by the concept, Jennie-Lou delved deeper into mid-term rentals, recognizing the potential for stability and sustainability that it offered. Her curiosity grew as she absorbed information about this untapped market catering to professionals, families, and individuals seeking temporary accommodation for weeks or months. Inspired by her friend Lisa's success in the field, Jennie-Lou made the bold decision to pivot her investment strategy toward mid-term rentals.

One day, while inspecting a potential investment property, she imagined how it could be transformed into a comfortable, home-like environment for a family in transition or a professional on assignment. This vision ignited her passion and fueled her resolve to succeed in the mid-term rental market.

Armed with knowledge and determination, Jennie-Lou meticulously planned her entry into the mid-term rental market. She sought out properties with features that would attract tenants seeking a comfortable, home-like experience during their temporary stay. Leveraging her expertise in property management, she ensured that each rental unit was meticulously prepared and maintained to meet the needs of her tenants.

She faced numerous challenges, from managing renovation budgets to navigating local regulations. But with each obstacle, she found a solution. She negotiated with contractors, learned zoning laws, and even spent weekends painting rooms to cut costs. Her resilience shone through each hurdle she overcame.

Though the transition was not without its challenges, Jennie-Lou's resilience prevailed. She tapped into the strength she had cultivated throughout her personal growth journey, and her setbacks became stepping stones for growth and improvement. She adapted her approach, prioritizing tenant satisfaction and building strong relationships within the mid-term rental community. Her networking efforts provided valuable insights and guidance from seasoned investors who had walked a similar path.

Jennie-Lou quickly recognized the importance of community in her new venture. She made an effort to connect with other mid-term rental investors, attending local meetups and even hosting a few herself. These gatherings gave her priceless insights into the intricacies of the mid-term rental market, and she found herself learning from others' triumphs and setbacks.

As her mid-term rental business started to prosper, Jennie-Lou's confidence skyrocketed. She began imagining even bigger possibilities. Opportunities for expansion beckoned, and she explored new markets and potential partnerships to help grow her operations and increase her impact. Her journey from overcoming self-doubt had become something much more profound and rewarding than she had ever dreamed.

Her success was evident not only in her financial achievements but also in the positive feedback from her tenants. A heartfelt thank you note from a family who had enjoyed their stay in one of her properties or a glowing review from a professional who had felt at home during their assignment validated her hard work and dedication.

Through relentless determination, unwavering self-belief, and commitment to personal growth, Jennie-Lou achieved financial independence and found a deep sense of purpose. Offering comfortable and welcoming homes to her tenants during their times of transition turned into more than just a business; it became a way to positively influence their lives.

She realized that her business wasn't just about providing accommodation, but also about supporting people during significant transitions in their lives. This insight brought a new level of satisfaction to her work.

Reflecting on her transformation, Jennie-Lou saw the value of self-compassion, celebrating victories, and challenging negative thoughts. These practices boosted her resilience and determination to face the inevitable hurdles and setbacks on her path.

She started incorporating daily affirmations into her routine, constantly reminding herself of her strength, resilience, and abilities. These affirmations became her daily dose of positivity, helping her maintain a balanced outlook throughout the highs and lows of her entrepreneurial journey.

With her journey serving as a testament to the power of perseverance and hard work, Jennie-Lou's story inspired others struggling with self-doubt and uncertainty. She realized that her experiences weren't just her own, but also resonated with anyone who had faced adversity, taken a leap of faith, or dared to dream of a better life. Her story became a beacon of hope and resilience, showcasing the indomitable human spirit, and encouraging others to overcome obstacles and reach for their dreams.

Jennie-Lou was eager to share her journey with others, believing that her experiences could serve as a guide for aspiring real estate investors. She began speaking at local seminars and online forums, offering advice and sharing the lessons she had learned along the way.

As Jennie-Lou continued to build her successful midterm rental business, she knew her story was far from over. The future held new challenges and opportunities, and she embraced them with the same unwavering belief and determination that had carried her through her journey thus far. With each step forward, she remained committed to personal growth, continuous learning, and the unwavering pursuit of her dreams.

The journey of Jennie-Lou is not just a tale of entrepreneurial success but also a testament to the power of resilience, self-belief, and determination. As she continues to explore new opportunities and expand her business, she stands as a beacon of hope and inspiration for anyone who dares to dream and has the courage to follow their passion, no matter the obstacles.

Through her story, Jennie-Lou hopes to inspire others to embrace their own personal growth journeys. She hopes to encourage others to face their fears, challenge their limitations, and dare to step outside their comfort zones. She continues to serve as a reminder that it is not the setbacks that define us, but how we rise from them and continue to pursue our dreams.

Her story sends a powerful message: that every struggle, every setback, is an opportunity to learn, grow, and become stronger. It tells us that we have the power to give our lives value, that we don't have to measure ourselves by anyone else's standards, and that by valuing ourselves for who we are, we can live fulfilling lives and reach our full potential.

At the end of the day, Jennie-Lou reminds us that showing up for ourselves is not always easy, but it is the best decision we can ever make. It enables us to grow as individuals, find a sense of purpose and direction in our lives, and become more confident, self-assured, and content than ever before.

So, if you are feeling lost or uncertain, remember Jennie-Lou's story. Show up for yourself. Focus on your own needs, dreams, and aspirations. Find your own voice and believe in your abilities. Most importantly, be kind to yourself and never stop learning and growing. Every day, make a choice to show up. Because as Jennie-Lou's journey shows, "No one is coming to save you!"

Key Insights:

1. The importance of taking a step back and reevaluating strategies after setbacks, allowing for discovering new opportunities and better aligning with personal values and passions.

2. Emphasizing research and education to better understand market trends and best practices, leading to more informed decisions and optimized success in one's chosen niche.

3. The power of perseverance, self-belief, and hard work in overcoming challenges ultimately leads to personal and financial growth.

Action Steps:

1. Reflect and Reevaluate: After encountering setbacks or disappointments, take a step back to reflect on your experiences and reevaluate your strategies. Identify areas where you can learn from past mistakes and consider new opportunities that align with your values and passions.

2. Research and Educate: Research and educate yourself about your chosen niche or area of interest. Attend seminars, join online forums, and reach out to experienced professionals for advice and guidance. Leverage this

knowledge to make informed decisions and optimize your chances of success.

3. Seek Growth and Expansion Opportunities: As you gain confidence in your chosen niche or area, explore opportunities for growth and expansion. Identify new markets, potential partnerships, and innovative strategies that can help scale your operations and multiply your impact.

Reflection: Reflect on a moment when you had to regroup and refocus your efforts after experiencing setbacks or disappointments. How have these experiences shaped your resilience, determination, and ability to adapt to challenges? How did you identify and pursue a new direction that aligned with your values and passions?

Chapter 12

Unleashing Possibilities: Rising Above Doubts and Discovering Financial Freedom Through Mid-Term Rentals

Jennie-Lou's path to financial freedom and personal fulfillment through mid-term rentals was a tumultuous yet rewarding journey. With each step, she experienced a mix of exhilaration and challenges that tested her resilience, determination, and passion for her newfound career. This chapter dives deep into the emotional rollercoaster of Jennie-Lou's story, highlighting the valuable lessons she learned from triumphs and setbacks alike.

As Jennie-Lou ventured into mid-term rentals, a mix of excitement and apprehension swept over her. In this significant moment, she stood on the edge of an uncharted path, her heart racing with anticipation. After facing setbacks in short-term rentals before, she couldn't help but feel a hint of anxiety about the possibility of failure. However, her unwavering determination and growing self-belief propelled her forward, outweighing any lingering doubts that occasionally crossed her mind. Still, she couldn't ignore the nagging question: Could she truly succeed in this new venture?

Her journey unfolded as Jennie-Lou acquired properties and undertook their renovation, targeting the ideal market for mid-term rentals. Along the way, she encountered a series of expected and unexpected challenges. Each day brought a new puzzle to solve, a fresh opportunity for innovation. Negotiating with contractors, navigating complex zoning regulations, and addressing unforeseen maintenance issues pushed Jennie-Lou out of her comfort zone. Yet, every obstacle served as a stepping stone for growth, providing invaluable lessons and chances to refine her approach. With each hurdle she overcame, Jennie-Lou's self-confidence soared, solidifying her belief in her ability to thrive in the mid-term rental market. Ultimately, these challenges not only tested her determination but also shaped her into the entrepreneur she was becoming.

During moments of uncertainty, Jennie-Lou made a conscious effort to maintain an optimistic mindset. She clung tightly to her vision of success, nurturing it with unwavering faith and tenacity. Practicing visualization techniques and daily affirmations anchored her focus and built her mental resilience. Additionally, she started keeping a journal to document her thoughts, fears, and victories, finding solace in this practice as it served as an outlet for her emotions and a tangible record of her journey.

Jennie-Lou cultivated a supportive network comprising friends, family, and fellow entrepreneurs who shared her passion for real estate and personal growth to sustain her motivation during challenging times. This community, her tribe, became her backbone, their belief in her fueling her perseverance. Their unwavering support, encouragement, and camaraderie became invaluable pillars as Jennie-Lou navigated the unpredictable real estate investing landscape. Together, they celebrated successes, offered advice, and provided the unwavering support that kept Jennie-Lou moving forward. While there were moments when she felt overwhelmed, the shared stories and experiences from her network often provided the solace and motivation she needed to continue on her path.

Jennie-Lou's journey toward financial freedom and personal fulfillment through mid-term rentals was a tumultuous yet rewarding experience. With each step, she encountered a mix of exhilaration and challenges that tested her resilience, determination, and passion for her newfound career. This chapter delves deep into the emotional rollercoaster of Jennie-Lou's story, highlighting the valuable lessons she learned from both triumphs and setbacks.

As Jennie-Lou ventured into mid-term rentals, a wave of excitement and apprehension washed over her. Having previously encountered setbacks in short-term rentals, she couldn't help but feel a twinge of anxiety about the potential for failure. However, these previous experiences were not in vain; they served as the necessary catalyst for her to explore new avenues in real estate. Her unwavering determination and growing self-belief propelled her forward, outweighing any lingering doubts that occasionally crept into her mind.

The journey unfolded as Jennie-Lou acquired properties and embarked on their renovation, targeting the ideal market for mid-term rentals. Along the way, she encountered a series of expected and unexpected challenges. She battled against stringent deadlines and struggled to manage multiple projects concurrently. Negotiating with contractors, navigating complex zoning regulations, and dealing with unforeseen maintenance issues stretched Jennie-Lou beyond her comfort zone. Yet, each obstacle served as a stepping stone for growth, providing invaluable lessons and opportunities to refine her approach. With every hurdle she conquered, Jennie-Lou's self-confidence soared, solidifying her belief in her ability to thrive in the mid-term rental market.

During moments of uncertainty, Jennie-Lou consciously tried to maintain an optimistic mindset. She practiced visualization techniques and daily affirmations to anchor her focus and build her mental resilience. She found solace in the words of her favorite authors and entrepreneurs, whose words of wisdom often served as a source of comfort and inspiration. She wrote down these pearls of wisdom and revisited them whenever she needed a morale boost. Additionally, she set SMARTER goals that were specific, measurable, achievable, relevant,time-bound, evaluated, and reviewed goals, allowing her to track her progress and celebrate milestones along the way.

Jennie-Lou cultivated a supportive network comprising friends, family, and fellow entrepreneurs who shared her passion for real estate and personal growth to sustain her motivation during challenging times. She created a virtual community where she and her peers could share their experiences and insights, fostering a collaborative environment that benefitted everyone involved. Their unwavering support, encouragement, and camaraderie became invaluable pillars as Jennie-Lou navigated the unpredictable real estate investing landscape. Together, they celebrated successes, offered advice, and provided the unwavering support that kept Jennie-Lou moving forward.

The journey was not without moments of pure joy and exhilaration. Jennie-Lou experienced profound satisfaction as she witnessed her newly renovated properties come to life, filling with grateful tenants who appreciated the welcoming and comfortable spaces she had created. These moments fueled her passion, igniting a renewed commitment to her business and reinforcing the impact she could have on the lives of others while realizing her own dreams. She savored these moments, recognizing them as tangible proof of her progress and the successful manifestation of her vision.

With her expanding portfolio and flourishing business, Jennie-Lou began to taste the sweet fruits of financial freedom. Freed from the shackles of debt and the anxiety of living paycheck to paycheck, she relished knowing that her unwavering dedication and perseverance had paid off. This newfound financial stability also enabled Jennie-Lou to give back to her community and support causes close to her heart, amplifying the fulfillment she derived from her journey.

Throughout the emotional and exhilarating expedition toward financial freedom through mid-term rentals, Jennie-Lou discovered the significance of embracing the entire spectrum of emotions that accompanied her endeavors. Each experience, whether marked by triumph or challenge, played a pivotal role in her growth and evolution, molding her into the resilient, passionate, and successful entrepreneur she had become.

This chapter stands as a testament to the power of persistence, self-belief, and adaptability. By wholeheartedly embracing every facet of her journey, Jennie-Lou transcended challenges, extracted wisdom from setbacks, and ultimately achieved her dreams. Her story is a shining example of what is attainable when one dares to dream big, takes courageous action, and perseveres relentlessly in pursuit of greatness. It also emphasizes the importance of fostering a supportive network and maintaining a positive mindset, even when confronted with adversity.

Jennie-Lou's expedition toward financial freedom through mid-term rentals left an indelible mark on her life and the lives of those around her. Her triumphs inspire others, showcasing the transformative power of determination, self-belief, and the unwavering pursuit of dreams, no matter how audacious they may seem.

As her mid-term rental business flourished, Jennie-Lou began to experience a profound sense of purpose and fulfillment. Beyond providing a valuable service to her tenants, she was actively creating a legacy for herself and her family. The impact of her efforts resonated in the lives she touched, the smiles she ignited, and the transformations she witnessed in the properties she revitalized. This realization further fueled her passion and commitment to the journey.

Jennie-Lou continued to invest in her personal growth and development throughout her growth phase. Attending workshops, immersing herself in books, and seeking mentorship from seasoned real estate professionals became integral to refining her skills and expanding her knowledge. Her thirst for learning and her commitment to applying newfound insights enabled her to continually elevate her business and stay ahead in a competitive landscape.

Jennie-Lou's journey was not without moments of heartache and disappointment. Deals fell through, tenants unexpectedly departed, and unforeseen expenses threatened her financial stability. In such instances, Jennie-Lou leaned on her support network and the coping strategies she had developed throughout her journey. Reminding herself of her progress, the obstacles she had surmounted, and the dreams she was actively pursuing allowed her to maintain composure and resilience in the face of adversity.

One poignant episode within Jennie-Lou's journey involved a serendipitous encounter with a family facing dire circumstances. Jennie-Lou discovered their struggles through a community outreach program and felt compelled to make a difference. Moved by empathy and a desire to give back, she offered the family one of her rental properties. This act of kindness went beyond providing shelter; it breathed new life into a needy family, rekindling hope and offering respite from their relentless challenges. Witnessing the profound impact of her gesture ignited a renewed sense of purpose and gratitude within Jennie-Lou, further reinforcing the significance of her work.

This experience served as a poignant reminder that true success extends beyond financial gains. Jennie-Lou realized that staying true to her values, practicing empathy, and actively contributing to her community were integral to her journey. It inspired her to seek out further opportunities to uplift those in need, becoming a beacon of hope and support during their darkest moments.

Through this act of kindness, Jennie-Lou witnessed firsthand the transformative power of extending a helping hand and showing compassion to those in need. It reaffirmed her belief that success transcends personal achievements and resides in the positive impact made on the lives of others. Jennie-Lou carried this experience as a guiding light, constantly reminding her to remain true to her values and never lose sight of the profound impact she could make in the world.

Jennie-Lou's emotional journey through mid-term rentals was a testament to her strength, courage, and resilience. Her unwavering determination and refusal to succumb to adversity became a beacon of inspiration for others, showcasing the extraordinary power of unwavering determination, self-belief, and the relentless pursuit of dreams.

Ultimately, Jennie-Lou's story encapsulates a triumphant narrative of conquering self-doubt and adversity, demonstrating the transformative power of persistence and the undeniable impact that passion and purpose can have on one's life. This story resonates with all who have faced challenges, doubted themselves, or dared to dream big. Above all, it is a potent reminder that anything is achievable with the right mindset, a supportive network, and an unwavering commitment. As Jennie-Lou continues to build her business and extend her reach, she remains a symbol of hope and resilience, proof that the power to transform lives lies within us.

Key Insights:

1. Embrace the emotional journey: Pursuing financial freedom and personal fulfillment is often accompanied by emotional highs and lows. Embrace both the challenges and triumphs as they contribute to personal growth and the overall journey.

2. Enjoy the fulfillment of helping others: Financial freedom allows you to give back to your community and support causes close to your heart. This adds another layer of fulfillment and purpose to your journey.

3. Invest in personal development: Invest in your personal growth by attending workshops, reading books, and seeking mentorship from experienced professionals. This helps refine skills and expand knowledge, keeping you ahead of the competition.

4. Stay true to your values: During your journey, remember the impact you can make on the lives of others and stay true to your values. Acts of kindness and generosity uplift others and renew your sense of purpose and gratitude.

5. Be a beacon of hope and resilience: Use your story to inspire and motivate others to pursue their dreams and break through barriers. Your journey is a powerful reminder of what can be achieved with determination, self-belief, and unwavering commitment.

Action Steps:

1. Develop a plan: Create a detailed business plan outlining your goals, strategies, and timeline for achieving financial freedom in your chosen niche.

2. Educate yourself: Enroll in courses, attend seminars, read books, and seek advice from experienced professionals to deepen your understanding of the real estate market and your chosen niche.

3. Set SMARTER goals: Establish specific, measurable, achievable, relevant, time-bound, evaluated, and reviewed goals for your business. Regularly review and adjust them as needed.

4. Maintain a positive mindset: Practice daily affirmations and visualization techniques, and celebrate your achievements to help build mental resilience and stay focused on your goals.

Reflection: Reflect on your journey towards achieving your personal or professional goals. How have your experiences shaped your growth and ability to overcome adversity? How have you dealt with the emotional highs and lows that accompanied your progress? What strategies have you employed to maintain focus, resilience, and passion during challenging times?

Part IV: Empowering Transformation

Lessons Learned and Advice for Others

CHAPTER 13

The Power of Perseverance - Learning from the Journey

Jennie-Lou's inspiring journey to financial freedom and personal fulfillment through mid-term rentals is a testament to the power of perseverance. Jennie-Lou, a woman of petite stature with a vibrant smile that belied the challenges she faced, had a particular quirk of tapping her foot whenever she was deep in thought. In the face of countless challenges and setbacks, she never wavered in her determination to achieve her dreams. At one point, faced with a difficult tenant who refused to pay rent, Jennie-Lou felt overwhelmed. Yet, she navigated the situation gracefully and firmly, demonstrating her resilience.

In this chapter, we dive deeper into the crucial lessons that Jennie-Lou learned throughout her journey, offering insightful guidance for those embarking on their own paths of success and self-discovery.

During a stormy evening, Jennie-Lou found herself in her dimly lit office, contemplating a spreadsheet filled with numbers that made her head spin. She had recently experienced a significant financial loss on a property deal that had gone awry. However, instead of succumbing to despair, she chose to view it as a valuable learning experience rather than a reason to give up. Adopting this mindset cultivated resilience and strengthened her determination, using each failure as a stepping stone towards greater success.

Jennie-Lou was always an early riser, eager to seize the day. One morning, as she enjoyed her ritual cup of strong black coffee, she stumbled upon a new trend in the real estate market. Rather than dismissing it as a passing fad, she recognized it as an opportunity. Continually seeking new ideas, strategies, and perspectives allowed her to refine her business model and stay one step ahead of the competition.

Jennie-Lou also learned the power of having a clear vision and setting specific, measurable, attainable, relevant,time-bound, evaluated, and reviewed (SMARTER) goals. In a conversation with her mentor, she once said, "Without a clear vision, we're like ships sailing aimlessly in the sea." She maintained focus and motivation by articulating her aspirations and breaking them into actionable steps, even during the most challenging times. This approach enabled her to track her progress, celebrate her achievements, and adjust her strategies, propelling her toward her dreams.

During her regular weekend brunches with fellow entrepreneurs and friends, Jennie-Lou often discussed her business challenges and victories. "You are your company's best asset. Invest in your growth," one of her friends, a successful entrepreneur, once told her. These connections gave her valuable advice and insights and reminded her that she was not alone in her struggles and triumphs.

Jennie-Lou's journey also highlighted the importance of investing in personal development. She recognized that to succeed in her business, she needed to grow as an individual. As a result, she made a conscious effort to seek out resources, attend workshops, and pursue mentorship opportunities, which allowed her to expand her knowledge and enhance her skills. By prioritizing her personal growth, Jennie-Lou was better equipped to face the challenges that came her way and achieve her dreams.

In addition to these lessons, one day, while observing the sunrise after a night of working on a difficult property deal, Jennie-Lou realized something profound. She learned that success is not about avoiding obstacles or setbacks but pushing through them with unwavering determination. She scribbled in her diary that day, "The sun always rises, no matter how dark the night." She faced adversity head-on, repeatedly, refusing to let it deter her from her goals. This unshakable commitment to her dreams was ultimately the driving force behind her incredible achievements.

As Jennie-Lou's story unfolds, it becomes clear that her success is not a result of luck or circumstance but rather a product of her unwavering determination, resilience, and willingness to learn from her experiences. Her journey is a powerful reminder of the transformative power of perseverance, providing inspiration and encouragement to anyone seeking to overcome obstacles and achieve their dreams.

By sharing her journey and the lessons she learned, Jennie-Lou's story offers hope and guidance to others facing similar challenges or striving to realize their dreams. Her experiences testify to the power of perseverance, demonstrating that anyone can overcome adversity and achieve greatness with dedication, adaptability, and a supportive network.

As Jennie-Lou navigated the complexities of the mid-term rental market, she became increasingly aware of the importance of maintaining a healthy work-life balance. Her journey taught her that while dedication and hard work were essential to achieving her goals, it was equally important to prioritize self-care and nurture her relationships with friends and family. After a long day of work, Jennie-Lou would often retreat to her favorite spot in her house, a cozy nook by the window that overlooked a small garden. This realization led Jennie-Lou to develop strategies for managing her time and energy more effectively. During a Thanksgiving dinner with Lisa's family, Lisa's young niece asked her why she always seemed to be working. This innocent question was a wake-up call for Jennie-Lou and led her to learn how to delegate tasks and responsibilities, trust her team, and create boundaries between her personal and professional life. These practices improved her overall well-being and allowed her to maintain her passion and focus, ultimately contributing to her long-term success.

Another vital lesson Jennie-Lou learned was staying true to her values and principles. In the competitive world of entrepreneurship, it can be easy to lose sight of what truly matters and prioritize profit over people. However, Jennie-Lou recognized that her integrity and commitment to ethical business practices were the foundation of her success. By staying true to her values, she built a thriving business and cultivated a reputation for honesty and trustworthiness, ultimately attracting loyal clients and lasting partnerships.

Jennie-Lou's journey also revealed the power of gratitude and the importance of giving back. As her financial situation improved, she sincerely appreciated the opportunities and support that enabled her to achieve her dreams. This gratitude inspired her to pay it forward, using her resources and expertise to make a positive impact on her community and the lives of others. Whether through offering affordable housing solutions to those in need or mentoring aspiring entrepreneurs, Jennie-Lou's commitment to giving back added another dimension of fulfillment and meaning to her life.

Throughout her journey, Jennie-Lou learned the importance of celebrating her achievements and recognizing her progress. By reflecting on her successes and expressing gratitude for her milestones, she maintained a positive mindset and strengthened her determination, even during challenging times. These celebrations served as reminders of the incredible journey she had undertaken and the immense potential that still lay ahead.

Jennie-Lou's pursuit of financial freedom and personal fulfillment through mid-term rentals imparts invaluable lessons in perseverance, adaptability, and resilience. Her story exemplifies how obstacles can be overcome and dreams can be achieved through dedication, hard work, and a willingness to learn from both successes and failures. By sharing her experiences and the wisdom gained along the way, Jennie-Lou inspires and guides others on their own paths towards greatness, demonstrating that with the right mindset and support, anything is possible.

Reflection: Reflect on a challenging situation or setback in your life or career. How did you demonstrate perseverance, adaptability, and resilience during that time? What lessons did you learn from the experience, and how have those lessons contributed to your personal growth and your ability to overcome adversity?

Chapter 14

Embracing Failure - Turning Setbacks into Stepping Stones

Jennie-Lou experienced numerous setbacks, challenges, and failures throughout her journey to financial freedom and personal fulfillment. Instead of allowing these obstacles to deter her or undermine her confidence, she found solace in her grandmother's words, "Mistakes are the portals of discovery," a mantra she held onto during her darkest hours. This chapter explores Jennie-Lou's transformative mindset and the powerful impact of embracing failure as a stepping stone to success.

One key realization that allowed Jennie-Lou to turn her setbacks into stepping stones was her understanding that failure is an inevitable part of any journey. Rather than viewing her failures as evidence of her inadequacy or a reason to give up, she recognized them as essential components of the learning process. One late night, staring at her reflection in the mirror, she told herself, "You're learning, Jennie. It's okay to fail." This shift in perspective allowed her to approach each challenge with a sense of curiosity and determination, ultimately propelling her forward on her path.

In the early hours of the morning, Jennie-Lou would carefully examine documents, straining her eyes in the soft light as she faced the numerous challenges of her budding real estate venture. With each setback, she experienced disappointment, frustration, and self-doubt. However, she soon realized that dwelling on her failures only prolonged her suffering and hindered her progress. Instead, she made a conscious decision to reframe her experiences, focusing on the valuable lessons they offered and how they could contribute to her growth and improvement.

For example, when Jennie-Lou encountered difficulties in acquiring her first property, she sat down with a steaming cup of coffee, her brow furrowed with concentration, as she meticulously analyzed her approach, scrutinizing every detail of the unsuccessful transaction. She pinpointed areas for improvement and sought guidance from more experienced investors. By embracing her failure and using it as a catalyst for personal growth, she was able to develop new skills, refine her strategy, and ultimately secure her first successful real estate deal.

As her business grew, Jennie-Lou encountered even more challenges and setbacks. From dealing with difficult tenants and unexpected maintenance issues to facing fluctuations in the real estate market, she was constantly tested and pushed beyond her comfort zone. However, with each new obstacle, Jennie-Lou grew stronger, more resilient, and better equipped to handle future challenges.

One of Jennie-Lou's most significant setbacks was when she experienced a substantial financial loss on one of her properties. Initially, she was devastated, questioning her abilities and contemplating abandoning her real estate pursuits. However, after reflecting, she realized this failure was an opportunity for growth and learning. She analyzed the situation, identified her mistakes, and sought resources and mentorship to ensure she would avoid repeating the same errors in the future.

In addition to learning from her failures, Jennie-Lou also sought to learn from the experiences of others. She attended industry events, networked with fellow real estate investors, and read books and articles on her niche. This commitment to continuous learning allowed her to glean valuable insights and advice from the successes and failures of her peers, further equipping her with the knowledge and skills she needed to thrive in the competitive world of real estate investing.

Jennie-Lou's willingness to share her failures and lessons learned with others also profoundly impacted her personal and professional growth. By opening up about her struggles and the obstacles she had overcome, she could connect with others on a deeper level, foster meaningful relationships, and inspire those around her to embrace their challenges and setbacks as opportunities for growth.

Over time, Jennie-Lou's mindset toward failure evolved from fear and avoidance to acceptance and appreciation. She began to view her setbacks not as stumbling blocks but as stepping stones on her journey to success. This transformative mindset allowed her to face challenges with courage, resilience, and determination, ultimately contributing to her achievements in the mid-term rental market.

Jennie-Lou's story is a powerful reminder of embracing failure as an essential part of the journey toward success. She once said, "Failure isn't the opposite of success. It's part of success." This quote embodies Jennie-Lou's philosophy towards setbacks and reinforces the idea that embracing failure can lead to personal and professional growth.

Reflection: Think about a time when you experienced a setback or failure in your personal or professional life. How did your perspective on failure influence your response to the situation? Reflect on the lessons you learned from that experience, and consider how you could shift your mindset to view future setbacks as opportunities for growth and stepping stones toward success.

Chapter 15

Sharing the Light - Inspiring and Empowering Others through Jennie-Lou's Journey

As Jennie-Lou's journey unfolded and her success in the mid-term rental market continued to flourish, she became increasingly aware of the potential of her story to inspire and empower others. This chapter delves into how Jennie-Lou utilized her experiences, insights, and the lessons she learned along the way to help others overcome obstacles, achieve their dreams, and transform their lives.

Recognizing the impact of her own journey, Jennie-Lou felt a strong desire to share her knowledge and experiences with others. She understood the struggles and challenges that many aspiring entrepreneurs faced, as she had once been in their shoes. She believed her story could serve as a beacon of hope and inspiration for those navigating similar paths.

With this purpose in mind, Jennie-Lou embarked on a mission to illuminate the way for others. One of the ways she pursued this was through public speaking engagements. She became a highly sought-after speaker in the real estate industry, captivating audiences with her genuine authenticity and contagious passion. At a significant real estate conference, she took the stage and began to recount her journey - the hardships she faced, the triumphs she celebrated, and the invaluable lessons she learned. Her words resonated deeply with the audience, culminating in a powerful statement: "Every setback, every failure, is not a roadblock, but a stepping stone guiding you towards your ultimate destiny. Embrace them." The room erupted in applause, moved by her profound message.

Jennie-Lou also leveraged the power of social media to reach a wider audience. She shared her insights, tips, and experiences through blog posts, videos, and podcasts. In one memorable blog post, she candidly spoke about a deal that had fallen through. She detailed the emotional turmoil, the lessons learned, and how she bounced back, stronger and wiser. Her followers appreciated this transparency, leaving comments of gratitude and admiration.

But it wasn't all smooth sailing. Jennie-Lou faced her fair share of criticism and negativity as she navigated the public sphere. This was a new challenge - to maintain her authenticity while also protecting her emotional well-being. But Jennie-Lou was not one to back down. She believed in her message and its power to inspire change.

In addition to her speaking engagements and online presence, Jennie-Lou made a conscious effort to give back to her community. She volunteered her time and resources to support local organizations and initiatives, using her success to make a positive impact on the lives of others. Furthermore, she mentored aspiring entrepreneurs and real estate investors, offering guidance, encouragement, and wisdom gleaned from her experiences. One of her mentees, Rosa, managed to secure her first real estate deal under Jennie-Lou's guidance. This was a small victory, not just for Rosa, but also a testament to Jennie-Lou's impact.

One of the most powerful ways Jennie-Lou shared her light was by simply living her life as an example of what was possible. Her story demonstrated the power of resilience, perseverance, and self-belief, showing others that overcoming adversity, conquering self-doubt, and achieving extraordinary success is possible. Through her actions, Jennie-Lou embodied the transformative potential of embracing failure, learning from setbacks, and relentlessly pursuing one's dreams.

As Jennie-Lou continued to share her story, she witnessed its profound impact on others. She saw people inspired by her journey take courageous steps in their own lives, overcoming obstacles and achieving their long-held dreams. This realization only fueled her passion for making a difference even further.

Above all, Jennie-Lou's journey serves as a powerful reminder of the untapped potential within each of us. Her story showcases that anyone with determination, perseverance, and self-belief can overcome their challenges and achieve greatness. By sharing her light with the world, Jennie-Lou has inspired countless individuals to embark on their own transformative journeys, empowering them to realize their aspirations and unlock their full potential.

Jennie-Lou's unwavering commitment to inspiring and empowering others through her story has created a lasting legacy. Her impact has touched the lives of many, igniting a ripple effect of positive change. Her narrative, a testament to the transformative power of sharing one's light, continues to illuminate the path for countless individuals, inspiring them to boldly pursue their dreams and create meaningful impact in their own lives and the lives of others.

Reflection: Reflect on a time when someone else's journey, story, or experiences inspired you to make a positive change in your own life. What aspects of their journey resonated with you the most, and how did their story empower you to take action and overcome your obstacles?

CHAPTER 16

Advice for Others - Keys to Overcoming Obstacles and Achieving Success

As Jennie-Lou's journey culminates in personal triumph and financial freedom, she reflects on the lessons she learned and the wisdom she gained along the way. In this chapter, she offers advice to others who may be facing similar challenges, providing practical guidance and insights to help them overcome obstacles and achieve their goals. By sharing her experiences, she hopes to inspire and empower others to take control of their lives and realize their full potential.

Drawing from her own experiences, Jennie-Lou shares the following keys to overcoming adversity and finding success:

1. Develop a growth mindset: Embrace the idea that personal growth is an ongoing process and commit to continuous learning and self-improvement. Adopting a growth mindset

will make you more resilient in the face of challenges and more adaptable in pursuing your goals. Make it a priority to invest in your personal development by attending workshops, reading books, and seeking mentorship from those who have already achieved your goals. Adopting a growth mindset will make you more resilient in the face of challenges and more adaptable in pursuing your dreams.

2. Cultivate self-awareness: Take the time to understand your thoughts, emotions, and beliefs and how they may hold you back. Use journaling, meditation, or therapy to help you better understand yourself and uncover the hidden barriers preventing you from achieving your goals. By becoming more self-aware, you will be better equipped to recognize and confront your self-doubt, fears, and limiting beliefs.

3. Surround yourself with support: Seek out mentors, coaches, and a community of like-minded individuals who can provide guidance, encouragement, and motivation. A strong support system will help you navigate the inevitable challenges and setbacks along your journey. Be intentional about creating a network of people who share your values, goals, and aspirations and are genuinely invested in your success.

4. Set realistic goals and take consistent action: Break your goals into manageable steps and commit to consistently achieving them. Focusing on the small, attainable tasks will

build momentum and maintain your motivation. Utilize tools like SMARTER goal-setting and time management techniques to ensure that you stay on track and make steady progress toward your objectives.

5. Embrace failure as a learning opportunity: Recognize failure as a natural part of the journey and use it to learn, grow, and refine your approach. Adopt a "fail forward" mentality, understanding that every setback is an opportunity for growth and improvement. By viewing setbacks as valuable lessons rather than insurmountable obstacles, you will become more resilient and determined in your pursuit of success.

6. Maintain a positive attitude: Cultivate a mindset of optimism, gratitude, and self-belief. By focusing on the positive aspects of your journey and your potential for growth and success, you will be better equipped to overcome challenges and persevere through difficult times. Practice daily affirmations, visualization, and gratitude exercises to help you stay positive and maintain a healthy perspective on your journey.

7. Trust yourself and your abilities: Believe in your capacity to overcome obstacles, achieve your goals, and create your desired life. Trust that you deserve success and happiness, and have faith in your ability to make it a reality. Learn to

silence the voice of self-doubt and replace it with unwavering confidence and self-assurance.

8. Maintain balance and prioritize self-care: Ensure you prioritize your physical, mental, and emotional well-being as you pursue your goals. Make time for regular exercise, healthy eating, and relaxation to keep yourself energized and focused. Remember that true success is achieved when all aspects of your life are in harmony, so be mindful of maintaining balance in your personal and professional life

9. Stay persistent and never give up: Understand that the road to success is not always smooth and that obstacles and setbacks are inevitable. Remain persistent in the face of adversity and never give up on your dreams. Remember that every successful person has faced challenges along the way, and their determination and perseverance have ultimately led them to victory. Stay committed to your goals, and continue pushing forward, even when the going gets tough.

10. Celebrate your achievements and milestones: Recognize and celebrate your accomplishments along the way, both big and small. Acknowledging your successes boosts your confidence and motivation and serves as a reminder of your progress. Share your achievements with your support network, and take pride in the hard work and dedication that has brought you closer to your goals.

11. Be adaptable and open to change: Embrace that the path to success may not always be linear and may require you to adapt and change course. Be open to new ideas, opportunities, and strategies to help you achieve your goals more effectively. By staying flexible and open-minded, you can navigate unexpected challenges and capitalize on opportunities that may arise along the way.

12. Give back and help others: As you achieve success and reach your goals, remember the importance of giving back and helping others struggling along their journey. Share your knowledge, experiences, and resources to empower and inspire others to overcome their own obstacles and achieve their dreams. By paying it forward, you not only positively impact the lives of others but also enrich your own life with a sense of purpose and fulfillment.

Conclusion

Embracing Your Journey and Inspiring Others

Jennie-Lou's remarkable journey—from adversity to triumph—serves as a powerful testament to the resilience of the human spirit. Her story ignites a spark within us, urging us to rise above our circumstances, tap into our inner strength, and relentlessly pursue our dreams. The challenges that once threatened to consume her have now become stepping stones on her path to victory.

As we reflect on her experiences, we cannot help but be in awe of her audacious courage and unwavering determination. She fearlessly confronted her fears and limitations, demonstrating that adversity, when met with resilience, can fuel growth and transformation. Her story emanates hope, serving as a shining example that faith in ourselves, combined with hard work, can overcome the seemingly insurmountable challenges that life presents.

The profound wisdom of Proverbs 3:5-6 (NIV) deeply resonates with Jennie-Lou's journey, offering solace and guidance: "Trust in the LORD with all your heart and lean not on your own understanding; in all your ways submit to him, and he will make your paths straight." This spiritual insight provides us with the strength and comfort to navigate our own turbulent waters, keeping our heads held high and our hearts resolute

As we approach the end of this book, let us hold onto the spirit of Jennie-Lou as a compass, guiding us toward our dreams and aspirations. Like her, let us face our obstacles with unwavering determination, cultivate self-belief, and remain steadfast in our pursuit of success. Remember that every setback is an opportunity to rise stronger, and every failure is a lesson that propels us toward greater wisdom.

Moreover, Jennie-Lou's unwavering commitment to giving back and empowering others reminds us of the profound impact we can have on the lives of those around us. As you achieve success and financial freedom, seek opportunities to uplift and support others on their own journeys. Share your knowledge, experiences, and resources to create a ripple effect of positive change, inspiring others to embrace their potential and pursue their own dreams.

Remember, the power to create the life we desire lies within each of us. We are responsible for harnessing and using that power to shape our destinies and live fulfilling lives.

Let us embark on our journeys, unshackled from the chains of self-doubt and fear. With every step we take, let us remember Jennie-Lou's lessons and strive to become the best versions of ourselves. In doing so, we, too, can create a life of purpose, passion, and fulfillment. Let's remember that within us resides the power to shape our destinies and live lives rich in purpose and passion.

Echoing Jennie-Lou's powerful words, "Never give up on your dreams. No matter how impossible they may seem, remember that you have the power within you to overcome any obstacle and achieve greatness. Trust your journey, embrace your struggles, and believe in your limitless potential." This sentiment serves as a potent reminder of our innate strength and resilience.

And so, as we part ways with Jennie-Lou, let her story continue to resonate within our hearts and minds. May it be a daily reminder of our power to rise above our circumstances and achieve the life we deserve.

Resources:

As you embark on your journey toward personal growth, financial freedom, and real estate success, it is essential to equip yourself with valuable resources that can provide guidance, inspiration, and practical tools. The following resources have been carefully curated to support you in your pursuit of a fulfilling and prosperous life. Whether you seek knowledge on real estate investing, personal development, or financial literacy, these resources will serve as invaluable companions along your path to success.

Books:

1. "The 5 AM Club" by Robin Sharma - A transformative guide to personal growth and achieving peak performance. Start your day with intention and embrace the power of early morning rituals to boost productivity and create a life of purpose.

2. "Rich Dad Poor Dad" by Robert Kiyosaki - An influential book on financial literacy and mindset, providing insights into building wealth through real estate and other investments. Learn valuable lessons on the importance of financial education and adopting a wealth-building mindset.

3. "The Millionaire Real Estate Investor" by Gary Keller - A comprehensive guide to real estate investing, covering strategies, principles, and practical tips for success in the industry. Gain a deep understanding of the real estate market and learn how to build a profitable investment portfolio.

4. "The Power of Positive Thinking" by Norman Vincent Peale - An inspiring book that explores the impact of positive thinking and offers strategies for developing a positive mindset. Discover the transformative power of optimism and learn techniques to overcome challenges and attract success.

5. "The Success Principles" by Jack Canfield - A motivational book outlining principles and strategies for achieving personal and professional success. Learn how to set clear goals, overcome obstacles, and create a roadmap for reaching your full potential.

Online Courses and Programs:

1. Real Estate Investing Masterclass - A comprehensive online course that provides in-depth knowledge and practical tools for successful real estate investing. Gain insights into property analysis, financing strategies, and property management techniques from experienced industry professionals.

2. Personal Development and Mindset Mastery Program - A transformative program designed to help individuals develop a growth mindset, boost confidence, and unleash their full potential. Learn powerful techniques for personal growth, goal setting, and self-motivation. *Text the word "Mindset" to +1(833)248 -3147 to schedule a free 30 min consultation call to get started*

3. Financial Literacy Course - An educational program that covers essential financial concepts, including budgeting, investing, and building wealth. Develop a solid foundation in personal finance and gain the knowledge and skills to make informed financial decisions.

4. Property Management Certification Program - A specialized course that provides training and certification in property management, offering valuable insights into effectively managing real estate investments. Learn best practices in tenant screening, lease agreements, and property maintenance.

Websites and Blogs:

1. Mindful Entrepreneur (https://mindfulentrepreneur.medium.com/) - A blog exploring the foundations of leadership and mindset, providing insights

and guidance on becoming an exceptional leader and developing a powerful mindset.

2. BiggerPockets (www.biggerpockets.com) - A popular online community and resource hub for real estate investors, offering forums, articles, podcasts, and educational materials. Connect with like-minded individuals, access expert advice, and stay updated on industry trends.

3. Investopedia (www.investopedia.com) is a comprehensive financial resource website covering a wide range of investment topics, including real estate, stocks, and personal finance. Access articles, tutorials, and financial tools to enhance your financial knowledge.

4. MindTools (www.mindtools.com) - A platform offering a variety of resources and tools for personal and professional development, including articles, assessments, and online courses. Develop essential skills in leadership, communication, time management, and decision-making.

5. Entrepreneur (www.entrepreneur.com) - A leading publication and website providing valuable insights, advice, and inspiration for entrepreneurs and business-minded individuals. Stay informed about the latest trends, learn from successful entrepreneurs, and find practical tips for building a thriving business.

Remember that these resources are designed to complement your journey and offer guidance. Keep striving to broaden your knowledge and skills by exploring additional resources and seeking personalized advice when necessary. Stay dedicated to your personal growth and embrace the opportunities that await you. The road to success is built on continuous learning, perseverance, and a mindset that remains open to new possibilities.

Made in the USA
Las Vegas, NV
09 June 2023